A Sierra Club Totebook®

Hiking the Yellowstone Backcountry

by Orville E. Bach Jr.

Sierra Club Books • San Francisco

Copyright © 1973 by the Sierra Club.
Photographs by the author.
All rights reserved.
Library of Congress Catalog Card Number 72-96121.
International Standard Book Number 87156-078-X.

Third Printing, 1977.
Manufactured in the United States of America.

About the Book...

One of the many interesting things about the Yellowstone-Teton area is the close proximity of two parks that are so different. Once in the vicinity, it is almost impossible to go to one and not the other. We had originally planned to include trail guides to both areas in a single Totebook, but it was not long before we discovered that it would be difficult—even with two separate volumes—to keep them down to "jean-pocket size." But still, we felt it was unrealistic to deal with each park as a separate island. As a result, we have combined the authors' background information to both guides—*Hiking the Yellowstone Backcountry*, by Orville E. Bach Jr., and its companion volume, *Hiking the Teton Backcountry*, by Paul Lawrence—into a single introductory section which is included in both volumes. Our thanks to Eugene J. Walter Jr., who worked from the manuscripts and a number of reference books to provide the overview of the two parks. As you read through the text you will find that the geological history, weather information and sometimes the grizzly, do not stop at the boundary of Yellowstone, but continue into the Teton area. We thought that you probably would, too.

—the editors
Sierra Club Books

...And the Author

Orville Bach is a man of many interests. In 1968 he graduated from Auburn University in Alabama with a degree in economics and management. He is looking forward to a masters in physical geography. During his free time he has managed to hike the 1,000 miles of trails in Yellowstone.

Native southerners, Bach and his wife moved to the West late in the 1960's and worked as season employees in both Glacier and Yellowstone national parks. At present they make their home at Malmstrom Air Force Base in Great Falls, Montana. Eventually, he hopes to join the ranks of the Park Service permanently.

Preface

The management of Yellowstone National Park will become increasingly important in the future and will have numerous problems to contend with. Obviously, the main one will be how to continue to preserve Yellowstone's magnificent wilderness in the face of increased backcountry use. A few years ago not very many people ventured into Yellowstone's backcountry, but the summer of 1972 saw an unprecedented number of hikers and backpackers. Wilderness hikers in Yellowstone are now being rationed by means of backcountry use permits.

Although the National Park Service is appointed the vital task of managing and preserving the wilderness, the responsibility rests with each and every backpacker who travels the park. Almost all Yellowstone backpackers are very conscientious about preserving the wilderness, and leave behind no evidence of their presence other than footprints. But those few—and it only takes a few—who persist in leaving their mess behind present a grave problem. Such a person is referred to as a "heavy walker." The heavy walker hurts all of us. He degrades the quality of the wilderness by littering the land, and in some areas imposes limited use due to the constant clean-up required. A single heavy walker, through his carelessness, does more harm to the wilderness than a hundred light walkers.

Hopefully, you will seldom meet such an individual in Yellowstone's wilderness. If you do, take the opportunity to educate him. If you see someone tossing garbage, cutting green trees, fouling lakes and pools with dishwashing, or camping where not permitted . . . speak to him. In a polite way, try to explain the consequences of his misbehavior. Some campers are genuinely ignorant, and will readily respond and learn from a conversation with a friendly stranger. On the other hand, if such an individual is as rude to you as he was to the land, then he should be reported to park rangers.

When you do encounter trash in the backcountry, make an attempt to pack it out if at all possible, even though it is not your mess. There can be no question that Yellowstone National Park today contains some of the nation's wildest and most beautiful scenery. We must strive to ensure that it will remain a source of inspiration for future generations.

Acknowledgments

A special note of thanks is due the National Park Service in Yellowstone (particularly Jerry Mernin and John Stockert) for their assistance. I am deeply indebted to my wife, Margaret, who accompanied me on many trips through the park and who typed the entire manuscript. I am also indebted to my good friend Rod Busby, who has walked with me on almost all the park's trails. Without his help and assistance, this book would not have been possible. With Margaret and

Rod, and also Ron, Marci, Prudy, Kathy, Rich, and Charlie, I have fond memories of twilight and trumpeter swan on Grebe Lake; the flowing, slow-motion beauty of the Lower Falls from Lookout Point under the moonlight; the magnificent view from atop Hedges and Dunraven peaks; stars twinkling on the waters of Mary Lake; watching grizzly, bison, elk, and moose in Hayden Valley; sandhill crane flying low over the lovely Bechler Meadows sounding their eerie calls; the beautiful waterfalls of the Bechler country— Union, Colonnade, Iris, Ouzel, and Dunanda; standing in awed silence before Old Faithful's spectral plume at dawn; a rainbow over the snow from atop Big Game Ridge; catching cutthroat from the waters of the wild Upper Yellowstone River; the majesty of Yellowstone Lake from atop Saddle Mountain; a pink dawn at McBride Lake, and hiking over Bliss Pass in the pouring rain admist the rumbling thunder.

—Orville E. Bach Jr.
August, 1973

Contents

TRAIL DESCRIPTIONS

APPENDICES

Before You Set Out

By Eugene Walter
with Orville Bach

A Natural History of the Yellowstone-Teton Region

If animals could vote, there would be more places like Yellowstone National Park. Take the ducks, for instance. Flocks of mallards approach the park by riverway, hugging the water, refusing to become airborne targets. Then they reach the boundary. Invisible though that line may be, the birds lift off and fly into the peace they know is on the other side. It is there for us, too.

The land of Yellowstone (3,472 square miles) is mostly high, rolling, forested plateau bounded by mountains—the Gallatin and Madison ranges to the west, the Absarokas along the east. Six miles south of the Yellowstone border is the northernmost entrance to Grand Teton National Park (484 square miles) and the sky-high spires that gave the mountain range its name and a reputation as a climbers' paradise. Most visitors arrive in their 4 wheeled prisons, checking off a list of postcard sights as if they were touring a version of Disneyland. Pity. Because beyond the limited viewpoint of looping scenic roads are thousands of acres of wilderness—enough spectacular scenery to keep even the most dedicated explorers busy for years. It takes time.

It *took* time. Billions of years went into the creation of these unique landscapes. Yet many of the wilderness wonderments you walk among today have been there for only a few ticks on the geologic clock.

The Making of the Mountains

The Tetons are among the youngest mountains in the Rockies—less than 10 million years old (most of the others go back 50 million years). The crystalline peaks gleaming in today's sun had their origin deep under the earth's crust in Precambrian times. During the Early Precambrian, sedimentary and volcanic rock accumulated down there in great heat and under intense pressure. This material was recrystallized into gneiss and schist (or mica schist) and repeatedly folded into enormous, multi-colored layers. As the strata settled, fractures developed. The underground heated up again and volcanic action poured molten streams of pegmatite and pink and light-gray granite up into the cracks. This mixture ultimately cooled and solidified in those fractures to form cross-hatchings and rocky wriggles called dikes.

Eons passed, and the mountains eroded away to a rolling plain on the earth's surface—until some 600 million years ago when shallow seas swept over the area to deposit the sedimentary rock that still covers much of the range. During the next 500 million years the waters receded and returned periodically, each time leaving behind additional crusty layers of limestone and sandstone. As the climate slowly changed, the region stabilized into luxuriant jungles so that, about 50 million years ago, the area that is now Grand Teton National Park resembled the Florida Everglades.

In mid-Pliocene, the whole rocky melange that had been brewing for eons began an upward movement. The Teton fault shifted and colossal blocks of gneiss, schist, and granite arose, breaking through the crust of limestone and sandstone that had covered them for centuries. The tilted blocks gradually lifted. Since that time, the forces of erosion have carved the Tetons we see today.

As the rock mass uplifted along the whole 40-mile-long fault, myriad dikes were exposed. Perhaps the most intriguing that are visible today are the enormous, nearly vertical dikes of diabase, shaded from dark green to black. The biggest of these, on Mount Moran, ranges from 100 to 120 feet in thickness and extends 7 miles in length. Grand Teton's black dike is 40 to 60 feet thick and the one on Middle Teton, 20 to 40 feet thick.

Volcanic Activity

The formation of Yellowstone came somewhat later and with considerably more violence. A series of volcanic eruptions—the first 2 million years ago, the second about 1.2 million years ago—blasted pumice and ash over several 100 cubic miles. A third cycle of eruptions began 600,000 years ago. Molten rock, or magma, churned upward into underground basins, creating on the surface a dome-like mountain 50 to 75 miles across. As surface stone cracked, some of the lava spilled out across the landscape. Finally, after preliminary rumbling and smoking, a massive explosion of gas spewed tons of debris over the land as far as what is now Kansas and Nebraska, destroying every vestige of life in its path. Modern geologists estimate the force of this blast at 200 times that of Krakatoa, the modern record-holder.

Gas pressure eventually subsided and the flow of molten ash and pumice halted. The giant earth dome that had risen over the lava collapsed and became an elliptical crater, or caldera. The crater, measuring 50 miles in diameter (just

short of a world's record) has eroded and become overgrown with vegetation, but is still visible below Mount
Washburn.

Volcanic activity continued with leaks rather than blow-
outs. The material that trickled over the earth—sometimes
cutting a path 30 miles across—was mostly rhyolite, a blend
of quartz and feldspar that still covers much of Yellowstone. Some of the rhyolite solidified into a black or brown
glass known as obsidian. Thus, today's backpacker sometimes finds himself walking over black glass, as on the Shoshone Trail.

Eruptions continued with diminishing force until about
75,000 years ago. Between each of these cycles, trees
sprouted in the new volcanic soil, only to be destroyed by
the next series of subterranean upheavals. During some of
the less violent blasts, nearby trees were buried—and preserved—under clouds of ash, dust, and other debris. Their
death was the birth of Yellowstone's 40 square miles of
fossil forest—the world's largest. Many of the trees, like
some on Specimen Ridge, remain upright, a unique depar-
ture from the fallen logs of other petrified forests around
the world.

New water courses opened across the land where those
early forests were taking root, and a lake welled up inside
the giant crater. Its waters spilled over the rim to become
the Yellowstone River, which in turn cut a 26 mile gash
known as the Grand Canyon of Yellowstone. In one section
the river has long been (and still is) heated by magma deep
below the surface. The scalding water has boiled the canyon
walls for century after century, transforming the brown and
gray rhyolite into vivid yellow rock. Hence, Yellowstone.

A Glacial Facelift

It remained for ice to finish the work, giving Yellowstone and Grand Teton their more or less final shape. In the Pleistocene, temperatures dropped, great masses of snow and ice accumulated and, ultimately, enormous glaciers pushed forward and altered the landscape. The glaciers arrived in 3 major and several minor waves over a period extending from 350,000 to 9,000 years ago. Each time, Yellowstone was almost completely submerged under these ice oceans, in some places as deep as 3,000 feet. On several occasions, sheets of ice flowing south from the Yellowstone plateau, met and joined sheets moving from the east into Jackson Hole.

Over these thousands of years, the climate warmed periodically, causing the glaciers to melt and retreat; but when the temperatures dropped, the glaciers returned once more. Each time they left their mark. The ice run-off branched into the canyons, grinding the edges off those chasms and rounding out their floors. Yellowstone's Madison River Canyon was transformed from a sharp cleft into a U-shaped valley. About 30,000 years ago, ice that was several 1,000 feet thick filled Jackson Hole and gouged out more of the great dip of flat plain that is walled by the towering Tetons. In valley after valley, a combination of glacial battering, frost, and avalanches chiseled gentle slopes into sharp inclines. The same abrasive action sharpened mountain peaks and ridges above.

During the last major advance, approximately 9,000 years ago, glaciers streamed through the Teton valleys, depositing great masses of rock, gravel, sand, and other debris into terminal moraines. When the glaciers eventually melted, these moraines remained as natural dams to form several of the Teton area's major lakes: Jackson, Leigh, Jenny, Bradley, Taggart, and Phelps.

Glaciers are still to be seen in Grand Teton National Park. But they are small, essentially dormant. They are probably recent arrivals, not remnants of the ice monsters that once dominated this part of the earth. Backpackers can hike trails to both Teton and Schoolroom glaciers for a glimpse of the past.

Fire-Water

Hot magma remains under Yellowstone, ready to take advantage of faults in the surface. The most apparent manifestations of such thermal activity are the geysers and hot springs and sulfur pools and fumaroles, spouting, hissing, and bubbling throughout the area.

Mention Yellowstone and most people instantly conjure up an image of Old Faithful. It, and the more than 200 other geysers in Yellowstone, are the products of water from above meeting fire down below. Yellowstone gets a great deal of rain and snow, particularly at higher elevations. The Upper Geyser Basin's annual precipitation is 18 to 20 inches. Millions of acre-feet of this water run off in the park's rivers and streams. But a great deal of it first seeps into the earth through the porous volcanic rock. Some of it stops at the water table and returns to earth through cold springs. Much water keeps going deeper, possibly to 2 miles. Contact with hot rocks at these depths plus pressure from water above sends its temperature soaring over the boiling point, perhaps more than 500°F. But down there it can't boil. Nor can it turn to steam because there is too much pressure. It has to go somewhere.

The escape route is an extremely complicated subterranean plumbing system. As water rises through the rocky channels, pressure goes down, and the water begins to boil vigorously.

Whether or not this overheated liquid bursts forth in fountain fashion or emerges with a hiss and a gurgle as a garden variety hot spring, depends on a delicate balance between several factors: temperature, pressure, the nature of the conduits through which it is passing, and how much steam energy is left after the cooling-off process on the way up. The same variables determine what kind of a geyser it becomes: a gusher like Old Faithful—with 10,000 to 12,000 gallons per eruption—or a quiet splash.

Despite popular mythology about the park's star attraction, Old Faithful is neither the most punctual nor the most powerful. The interval between its discharge time can vary from 33 to 148 minutes. Old Faithful shoots its watery plume up 100 feet, occasionally 200. There is no shortage of geysers in Yellowstone, and some of the most intriguing are for the backpacker only, reachable by trail to some remote region, such as the Shoshone Geyser Basin.

The same is true of some of the lesser known hot springs. Name a color, and there's a pool to match it. Sometimes rings of several colors occur within a single pool. Light reflecting and refracting through the boiling waters creates a full spectrum of blues, greens, browns, grays, yellows, reds. Color in the walls of the well shades some and, in others, algae grow and impart their own hues. A few are colored by mineral particles in the water, such as Sulfur Cauldron and Black Dragon's Cauldron (iron oxide). Perhaps the most spectacular is Mammoth Hot Springs, not because of the color, but for what it has left behind. The water there has a high concentration of calcium carbonate. For centuries, it has percolated up through layers of limestone and deposited extensive travertine terraces that look like relics of some ancient marble castle.

Mud pots are the comedians of the thermal world. They offer as much variation in sound as they do in color—a cacophony of bloops and belches, wheezes and gurgles, and resounding splats as mud flops back into the natural vats after being spit as high as 6 feet in the air. Sulfuric acid— hot spring water mixed with sulfur in the escaping gases— breaks down rhyolites to create the muddy "paint" that fills these holes. The colors—whites, pastel pinks, grays, yellows—come from sulfur and iron compounds mixing with the clay.

Flora

Of the 2 park areas, Yellowstone is the more heavily wooded. About 80 percent of it is forest, and 80 percent of that is lodgepole pine. Apparently, the lodgepole took over because forest fires were good for them. Up to a point, that is. It takes fiery heat to pry open the cones the lodgepole deposits on the ground. The cones can then eject their seeds for sprouting. While fire wiped out other tree species, it helped the lodgepole to reproduce and move in where the others had fallen.

Conifers are now dominant in both parks, but no one is sure how most of the trees and plants got to this region. The experts think that at least some of the species traveled a circuitous route, riding the breeze and the glaciers.

A trek through the wild places of present-day Yellowstone and Grand Teton is like an excursion through a series of gardens, the more charming for their lack of formality. You can meander over a meadowland trail edged with a blue and purplish bouquet of larkspur, lupine, gentian, and elephanthead, patches of cinquefoil and buttercups, and fields of lilies sprinkled with sage. A wooded path will lead you past trees garlanded with pale lavendar clematis, stands of tall monkshood and blue harebells, starry asters, and brilliant fireweed. Luminescent mosses cloak the rocky banks of a mountain stream and, under an archway of shady alders, the soft earth yields a colorful congregation of pink monkeyflowers, scarlet paintbrush, mountain bluebell, ivory columbine, red and yellow coralroot, yellow senecio. If you want to be sure of the name of that blossom beside the trail, take along a field guide to flowers.

Fauna

Man has always been lured to the Yellowstone-Teton region more by animals than by anything else. Ancestors of many of today's wild species probably arrived via the land bridge that once spanned the Bering Strait to Asia. During the Ice Age, primitive hunters followed the mammoth to this area. Later, the Indians pursued bison, elk, and deer along the slopes and through the valleys. The first full-time human residents we know of were mountaineering Indians who stalked bighorn sheep. The earliest white men were obsessed with the beaver whose luxurious fur made it a natural resource to be exploited.

Most people today regard this part of the world as bear country. Small wonder. The black bear is the only sizable animal most people are likely to see. Generations of heedless tourists encouraged the bear to depart from his natural habits and become a clownish, roadside alms-seeker and campground scavenger. Fortunately, the situation has improved somewhat today.

Then there are the others the tourists have no desire to meet: the grizzlies. Actually, there are only about 250 spread around Yellowstone (each requires a lot of space) and a mere handful south of the park in the Teton Wilderness. Fierce and fearless, the grizzly has all the equipment necessary to be king in these parts: bone-crushing jaws, razor-sharp, 6 inch claws, and amazing speed for a bulky, lumbering, 600 pound animal. There is nothing subtle about a grizzly bear, yet there is nothing quite so winsome as the springtime sight of a grizzly leading her cubs across Yellowstone's Hayden Valley in a search for roots and berries.

One of the best places to see wildlife, grizzlies included, is on Yellowstone's central plateau: Hayden Valley and the meadows along the banks of the Firehole, Madison, and Gibbon rivers. These grasslands are home to the elk, or wapiti, most numerous of the region's large animals. In the summer, there are up to 15,000 in Yellowstone alone.

The smaller mule deer is also here, grazing the valleys and forest edges. The pronghorn, America's only antelope, prefers the plains but occasionally ventures into open slopes of the valleys. Seeing one for more than a few seconds may take some doing since they are as speedy as they are skittish.

In the high meadows of the central plateau is the bison. This shaggy, bearded beast is a symbol both of man's folly and his enlightenment. At their peak, vast herds totaling 50 million animals ranged across the continent from western New York to Oregon and from Canada to Mexico. The Indians always hunted them, but without seriously depleting the population. When the white man opened the West, the buffalo suddenly fell victim to hungry railroad workers, hunters (a good "professional" could bring down 250 a day), and the U.S. Army, which embarked on a campaign to exterminate troublesome Indians by exterminating their food. By the late 1850's, the 50 million had dwindled to an estimated 540—most groups owned by conservation minded individuals. A few remained in Yellowstone.

In 1905 a group of concerned conservationists founded the American Bison Society to lobby for rigid protection laws, to arouse the public, to establish preserves, and to set up the nucleus of a breeding herd. The society was successful on all fronts and was eventually able to restock protected refuges at several points in the west. Now there are about 12,000 in the U.S., including Yellowstone's 800.

Moose, the only other really large creatures hereabouts, are to be found mostly in the wetlands, occasionally feeding along hillsides. Look for them on the Yellowstone River downstream from Yellowstone Lake, or at Avalanche Canyon in the Tetons. Marshlands also supply food and nesting grounds for the North American trumpeter swan. Like the bison, these birds were once on the verge of extinction. Only 70 remained at one point but, given protection, they have come back to number 100 in the park. Mountain marshes, ponds, and lakes are home as well to the muskrat, mink, otter, beaver, sandhill crane, great blue heron, osprey, and a variety of ducks, geese, and coots. The Molly Islands in the Southeast Arm of Yellowstone Lake are the only breeding grounds in a national park for the white pelican. Gulls, terns, and cormorants also nest on these rocky islets.

A climb to higher elevations—say, to Yellowstone's

Mount Washburn—may be rewarded by the sight of bighorn sheep along the ridges. And bald and golden eagles may also be seen launching themselves from rocky crags to soar over the valleys in search of food.

Any visit to the park interior is a birdwatcher's delight. More than 200 species have been identified. Warblers, juncos, kingfishers, nuthatches, goldfinches, flycatchers, swallows, hummingbirds, tanagers, chickadees. . . . This is another cataloguing operation that is better done on foot with the help of a pocket-sized field guide.

Park animals are protected from man but not from each other. The aim now is to give equal rights to predators and restore the balance of life. An earlier misguided policy held that eliminating predators would be good for the deer. It wasn't. Deer herds became over-populated, which nearly starved them out. It isn't nice to fool around with Mother Nature.

The unjustly maligned coyote patrols valleys, mountains, forests, meadows, or marshes keeping things tidy. If it weren't for coyotes, the parks would be overrun with mice, gophers, and rabbits. Smaller carnivorous critters—red fox, lynx, mink, wolverine, badger—are a secretive lot, difficult, but not impossible to spot. There are not many wolves or mountain lions and they, too, are shy about meeting people. With good reason.

Weather

Month to month, the climate is rather similar in Yellowstone and Grand Teton; but the latter generally takes you to higher elevations. Once you've passed the timberline, there are few places to hide. Even after clear, sunny days, the nighttime temperature at these heights dips close to freezing.

June

Each month has its advantages and disadvantages. If the high country is your goal, better wait till midsummer. Winter weather persists above 6,500 feet through May. June is still wintry above 8,500 feet. At slightly lower elevations, the bulk of the wilderness is frequently too soggy to do extensive hiking for at least the first 3 weeks of June. Slushy snow and high water make it inaccessible.

June can be ideal for traveling the shorter trails of the 2 parks. Newly blossoming wildflowers line paths through the valleys. Waterfalls, refreshed by melting snows, are at the peak of their beauty. The mountains are still capped with white. Most of the migratory birds are back and there's a flurry of nest building. Mule deer fawns are usually born in June. It's easier to see wildlife in general. Perhaps the best reason for going is that few tourists have arrived. June is wonderfully unpredictable. Every day of your visit could be clear and sunny. It might rain every day. It could snow.

July

July is more inviting to the backpacker. Days are generally brighter, brisk, seldom chilly. Nights are cold, particularly in the Tetons. In the mountains there are thunderstorms and stiff winds almost every afternoon; sometimes snow. But it should all pass in 1 or 2 hours. Patience.

When the water goes down late in July, fishing is at its best. Wildflowers are blooming at higher elevations. As the weather warms, some of the wildlife retreats up the slopes to mountain meadows. There are still many elk in the river valleys and moose in the bogs. The pelicans and gulls on the Molly Islands are scooping up fish for their newborn chicks. This is the month when fledglings of almost every bird species try their wings, and the trumpeter swans lead their young to water.

July is also the time when the bugs wake up. There are clouds of mosquitoes around marshes, lakes, meadows; any place where the snow has just melted. And they bite and bite and bite. Colder temperatures make them inactive. So they rest up at night for the next day's feast. If the mosquitoes neglect any part of you, an assortment of other insects are ready to help. It's imperative that you carry the proper repellent, creams, clothing, and netting for your tent.

August

In many ways, August is the prime month for backpacking excursions. Weather is dependable except for occasional thundershowers, especially high in the Tetons. Days are hot, nights are refreshingly cool, sometimes cold. The snow

is gone, the water has receded, trails are in great shape. The
mosquitoes and their pestiferous brethren have subsided
considerably. Above the timberline, alpine vegetation flowers briefly. In the forests, young birds declare their indepen-
dence of the nest.

September and Later

For many backpackers, September is the *only* time for Yellowstone and Grand Teton. Wildflowers are disappearing
but the trees are touched with color. Scarlets and golds
appear on the high slopes and seem to drift down toward
the valleys as the month goes on. The groves of aspen
acquire their golden glow.

Ponds and lakes are filled with ducks and geese stopping
over on their way south. Flocks of songbirds pause here on
their migrations. The insects are gone. So are most of the
people.

The big game is at its best. The ones that moved into the
mountains for the summer, like the bison, are returning to
the valleys. The grizzly is even handsomer, bundled in his
heavy winter coat. With a lot of luck you may spot a ma-
ture "silvertip." Its fur has a frosty appearance, the result
of light coloration on the tips of the hairs. Deer, elk, and
moose are living trophies, their racks of antlers matured to
magnificence, their coats thick as they glisten with a new
sheen in the autumn sunlight. For the elk, this is the time
of the rut or mating season. The bull elk announces his
intentions by bugling a high, piercing shriek that descends
to a booming, low grunt—a sound you won't forget.

In September, the wilderness is wild. So is the weather,
which becomes unpredictable. Rain is common, snow is
likely. But, while caution is necessary with snow, it isn't

quite the same problem as early in the season because it hasn't had time to accumulate in great depths.

Winter

Because of the ever-increasing popularity of snowshoeing and cross-country skiing in winter, it is appropriate to include some information on Yellowstone's winter possibilities.

Yellowstone's trails are identified by metal orange markers located well above snow level, so route-finding is easy. The only park road open in winter lies between the North Entrance and Cooke City, outside the Northeast Entrance. There are several ski-touring possibilities from there. Short trips include the Yellowstone River and Hellroaring Creek area, the Blacktail Deer-Plateau area, and the lower portions of Specimen Ridge and the Lamar River Valley. A longer trip would include the Slough Creek Valley up to the northern boundary—a trip of about 13 miles from the highway. For more extensive touring you may want to consider the Lamar River Trail down to Cold Creek Junction. From here there are several possibilities for a loop hike back to the Mammoth-Northeast Entrance Road. Other possibilities include skiing into Old Faithful from the West Entrance and extensive loop trips from the South Entrance. Several interesting trails originate from the Old Faithful area.

Patrol cabins may be available for shelter to small parties on some ski-touring trails. Arrangements must be made in advance with the Chief Ranger's office.

Before embarking on a cross-country winter trip, full consideration should be given to the severe elements. Yellowstone country is often the coldest in the nation—lows of minus 20°F. are common. It is essential that persons entering the winter wilderness be properly equipped and have sufficient experience and training to withstand such excursions under arduous conditions. A special permit from the Chief Ranger's office is required for overnight trips, and it is mandatory to have your plans reviewed, as current information—on potential avalanche areas, for example—is important.

For more information on a Yellowstone winter, obtain a copy of *Winter Comes to Yellowstone* from the Yellowstone Library and Museum Association, Box 117, Yellowstone National Park, Wyoming 82190. The cost is 35 cents.

Clothing and Equipment

Your Wilderness Wardrobe

Underfoot: For day hikes over relatively smooth, well-traveled trails, a light trail shoe is sufficient. But, where you will encounter rocky terrain, snow and ice, a heavy boot is advisable. Whatever the weight, certain specifications are in order:

- Sturdy, rock-resistant leather throughout.
- Rubber lug soles.
- Reinforced heel and toe.
- Protective padding of soft leather around the ankle for support, warmth, and comfort. (Be sure there's enough room for heavy socks inside.)
- A long, padded tongue.
- Waterproofing. (Remember to re-waterproof between backpacking expeditions.)

Once you have the boots, break them in gradually. Wear them around the house; take walks outdoors. Always wear the kind of socks you're taking on the trip. The boots are broken in when you can walk all day with a full pack over all kinds of terrain without sore feet. Clearly, this isn't something you wait to do until 2 days before the trip.

If your projected route includes streams without bridges, it's advisable to have an extra pair of light-weight shoes handy: sneakers or mukluks. A change before fording saves your boots and keeps your feet dry. Before you bed down for the night, remember to turn your boots upside-down to keep the moisture out.

Inside the boots, traditionalists prefer good old heavy woolen socks—warm and cushiony. You may want a light cotton inner-sock if they're scratchy. New terry stitched socks made of synthetic fiber and cotton can equal wool in warmth and cushioning. The air pockets in the looser weave also insulate better, keep feet dryer, and eliminate the need for inner socks. Terry stitched thermal socks are available in wool.

Inside: You may find yourself a bit less fastidious in the wilderness, but, if you insist on changing underwear every day, accept the fact that you'll have to do more laundry along the trail. Three extra sets is ample. Consider taking a set of long johns (cotton or wool).

Outside: Wear warm, long pants made of wool or cotton twill. Be sure the legs fit loosely. Tight legs get hot and bind up; awful if they get wet. Walking shorts—also loose-fitting—are a nice option when the weather heats up.

You'll probably want to spend most of the day in a cotton or light wool shirt. For cooler temperatures you'll need something more. Wool sweaters are not such a hot idea. They are too bulky and they don't offer enough options to adjust for changing temperatures. A heavy wool shirt or a light down jacket is better. A good wool sheds water and stays warm even when wet, but it adds weight and bulk. A zippered nylon/down jacket insulates well and lets moisture escape; it's light and compressible. However, if it should get soaked, it takes a long time to dry out. For early and late in the season, a heavier down jacket is recommended.

Take wool mittens and a cap if you're going early or late in the season. A hat will protect you from rain, cold and sun.

A poncho is the world's greatest portable shelter and one of the most essential items on your list. If you're caught in heavy rains or wicked winds, you can poke your head through the center, drape the big waterproof rectangle over you and either wait till the weather blows over or flap along the trail like a big bat. Your poncho does multiple duty: a rain fly for your tent, an emergency tent along the trail, a ground cloth, a cover for your sleeping bag on extra misty nights. Spend the money for a poncho made of tough, lightweight nylon coated with plastic resin. The inexpensive sheet-plastic variety won't hold up through many trips. Get one big enough to cover your pack frame as well as yourself (100 by 70 inches).

Backpacks

On day hikes, you can use a summit pack or rucksack. For a longer trip, you should have a pack mounted on a metal frame. Magnesium frames are becoming more popular than aluminum because magnesium is lighter yet just as strong. Make sure the frame is the right length to fit comfortably on your torso. It should curve along your spine. Get one with a padded waist belt and test it with a loaded pack. A proper frame will hold the load high so the weight is directed down through your hips to your legs. Padded shoulder straps are more comfortable.

The best packs are made of waterproof, nylon duck. The easiest to organize have strips of fabric inside that divide the pack into vertical or horizontal compartments. Look for plenty of zippered pockets on the outside to stow maps and other small items you want to get at quickly.

Sleeping Bags

In this part of the world, any summer night can be cold. The lightweight summer sleeping bag that kept you cozy in the Catskills will not serve you so well out west. The minimum you should figure on for Yellowstone and Grand Teton is a bag that will keep you warm in 30°F. That should suffice for the latter part of June through most of August. From mid-May to mid-June and the last week of August to mid-September you will need a bag for 20°F. Earlier or later, a 10°F. bag is necessary. These are general standards. What you choose naturally depends on your own ability to adjust to cold. For the sake of long-range flexibility, it may make sense to get the 10°F. bag (for which you will pay more). Unzipped, it can be comfortable up to 60°F. When it's warmer than that, you can open the bag over you like a blanket instead of crawling inside.

The critical element in your comfort is the guts of the bag: the filler. The one that offers the best combination of insulation, light weight, and compactness is goose down, an excellent insulator. Its fluffiness traps warm air more efficiently than any other filler. Duck down and synthetic foam (bulky but light) are reasonable compromises.

The factor that contributes most to warmth is the "loft" of the down, meaning the thickness of the sleeping bag after you fluff it out and lay it on a flat surface. That thickness creates insulating power. A 6 inch loft is proper for a bag that has a 10°F. rating. The finest quality goose down is the most expensive because it holds its loft longer than the cheaper grades. Warm toes are worth almost any price. Figure on spending $80 or more for a good quality goose down bag.

The other major considerations in your choice of a bag are lightness (4 pound maximum) and outer material (get tightly woven, water-repellent, rip-stop nylon). The exact type of construction is not vital so long as the down is spread evenly through the bag by a series of baffles, or tubes, sewn around the circumference of the bag (not lengthwise). Without the baffles, the down will shift and settle in one spot. Style is a matter of personal preference. The mummy bag with its hood is the snuggest. If that's too confining for you, get a semi-rectangular bag that spreads out more.

Having invested in a good sleeping bag, take good care of it. Put something between it and the ground, or it will soak up moisture. It dries *very* slowly. Freshen it with sun and air every morning before you repack. For added comfort you may want to bring a foam pad to put under your sleeping bag.

Tents

In this region a tent is not a luxury. Heavy rain, snow, sleet, and high winds can occur with little warning. Obviously, you want a tent that burdens you as little as possible, while supplying maximum protection. A 2-man tent shouldn't add more than 5 pounds to your load. Figure 8 pounds as the maximum for a 3-man shelter.

Tents constructed with a double layer of coated nylon are more expensive than those made with a single layer. Moisture condenses on the tent *inside* the single layer and drips, turning your sleeping quarters into a shower. Double layer tents are made with 2 sheets of fabric sewn together so that the moisture trickles down the outer layer, not on you. Your tent should be equipped with completely enclosed mosquito netting. That, too, adds to the cost.

In midsummer at lower elevations, you can usually get by with a minimal tent. The tube tent, a thin, 9 foot polyethelene tube, is available in 1- or 2-man sizes. You can also use a tarp. Take about 50 feet of braided nylon parachute cord to string up your tent. If your tarp doesn't have grommets, you'll need clamps. Tubes and tarps will keep out the rain, but they present no barrier to mosquitoes or biting flies. High winds can demolish them. In the high country, they are totally inadequate.

Filling Your Pack

Some of the items that belong in your pack don't fit into a category.

- Sunglasses. (Essential above timberline and in snow and ice. Sunlight becomes intensely bright in the clear, thin air.)
- Suntan lotion.
- Lip salve.
- Insect repellent.
- Swiss army knife.
- Small flashlight. (No telling what you'll have to find in the dark. It can also be used for emergency signalling. Tape the switch when it's in your pack so it doesn't turn on.)
- Toothbrush. (A little box of bicarbonate of soda is lighter, more compact, and more effective than toothpaste. A small spool of dental floss will also keep your teeth from rotting. Or carve yourself a tooth-

pick from a twig.)

- Soap. (Not detergent. Liquid biodegradable. In a plastic squeezebottle with a leak-proof spout. Use that 1 soap for every cleaning job.)
- Toilet paper. (Unrolled from the tube and rerolled flat and tight. Keep it in a plastic bag. Use it sparingly.)
- Plastic bags. (For lots of things that crop up, including the garbage you take out.)
- Canteen. (Not an absolute necessity. In this region running water is generally not far away.)
- Compass.
- First aid kit.

Optional:

- Small terry cloth face towel.
- Comb or hairbrush. (No telling who you'll meet on the trail.)
- Candle. (In case the flashlight breaks, and for lighting stoves.)
- Binoculars.

Now that you have all the equipment you *want*, eliminate everything you *don't need*. If you're new at this, even packing may require some practice.

Food

Fires in the back country can be dangerous and—without special permit—illegal. If you want to cook you will need a stove. Compact butane-cartridge stoves, like the Bleuet, are easy to operate. Gasoline stoves—the Svea, the Optimus—are better in cold weather, but it takes a certain amount of priming and pumping to light one.

Your kitchen:

- 1½ or 2 quart pot. The lid can double as a frying pan or plate.
- Plastic or metal cup.
- Spoon.
- Bowl for mixing or eating (optional).
- Bottle to mix powdered drinks.
- Spatula if fried foods are on the menu.
- Scouring pads for clean-up.
- Waterproof stick matches in a waterproof container.

Breakfast: Remember what your mother told you: eat a good breakfast. Her advice was never truer than on the trail. For juices, Tang is the best combination of taste and low cost. Orange and tomato juice crystals taste good but cost much more. To warm yourself, freeze-dried or instant coffee, or instant cocoa are good. Mixed together, they make a pleasant mocha drink. Powdered milk is another one of those compromises you accept in backpacking. Milkman is more palatable than most brands because a small amount of cream is added to it. Perma-Pak is the richest. You can even reconstitute it as cream. Both brands are packaged in convenient 1 quart containers. Remember to take sugar.

On cold mornings instant oatmeal or other hot cereals make a nutritious meal. Granola is filling in the stomach but heavy in the pack. Raisins, dates, and various freeze-dried fruits flavor up any cereal, hot or cold.

Freeze-dried eggs are an enormous improvement over the old-fashioned powdered eggs. Wilson's bacon bar is an excellent source of protein. Jerky (dried beef) is an equally good protein supplier.

Lunch: As a foundation for most trail lunches, depend on jerky and gorp, that unfortunately named but highly palatable and nutritious blend of raisins, seeds, dried fruits, nuts, and chocolate.

You can vary your lunches with hard cheese and unsliced salami. (On lengthy trips, salami may get a little ripe.) Try breads and crackers such as Mount Logan Bread and Pilot Biscuits. Canned butter (Darigold) will keep without refrigeration. Or spread your bread with dehydrated cheese or peanut butter. Dehydrated salads are available: tuna, potato, or egg.

Wash it all down with tea or lemonade or other fruit drinks. Wyler's fruit-ades are generally favored. Pem bars are a good finish to a lunch. If you'd rather have chocolate, Hershey's tropical bar won't melt.

Dinner: Soup helps to replace liquid you've lost during the day. It's also nourishing and takes the chill off the evening.

There are many possibilities for the main course with today's wide variety of freeze-dried entrees. Wilson's Meat Bar weighs 3 ounces. No refrigeration or cooking is necessary. Dice it and add to vegetables, noodles, or rice for a quick, tasty mulligan stew. Mountain House beef patties, pork patties, and meat balls are ready 1 minute after you add boiling water. (They are packed in cans which you should take out with you.) Avoid steaks and pork chops. They are too difficult to rehydrate thoroughly, and you'll have to carry a frying pan and oil to cook them. There is an extensive variety of freeze-dried and dehydrated vegetables and desserts.

Many people enjoy harvesting fruit that grows along the trail at various times during the summer: blueberries, huckleberries, raspberries, serviceberries, thimbleberries. It means expending extra time and energy but, if you find them, they make delightful desserts and delicious additions to breakfast. Know what you're picking. Not every bright berry is edible.

Snacks: This is one time you *should* nibble between meals. Your nibbles should have food value to supply extra protein, recharge your energy quickly (with easily assimilated sugars), and to replenish water you've lost through perspiration.

The ever-popular gorp is your most likely trail food. Also helpful: nuts, dried fruits, seeds, fruit sticks, hard candy, and drink mixes.

The feeding schedules you normally follow go out the door when you do. In the wilderness eat when you're hungry.

At all times throughout the day, drink plenty of liquid. During the hottest part of the summer, a supply of salt tablets is advisable. Nutritional needs are an individual thing. If you have any doubts, talk to your doctor. A small container of multi-vitamin capsules or vitamin C capsules might be in order.

In General . . . Any dish that needs more than 30 minutes of preparation should be left behind. The repeated emphasis on speed is especially pertinent on trips to Yellowstone and the Tetons. The higher you go, the lower the boiling point of water. When you hit 8,000 feet, it takes twice as long to cook as it does at sea level. Remember also that food digests more slowly at high altitudes. Frequent meals are better than a lot at once.

Plan ahead. If you average out to a pound or a pound-and-a-half of dry food for each day, you're on target. Become a food packager. Pack each item in the quantity desired for each meal. Many main courses are already packed in suitable single-meal containers.

Don't forget the salt and pepper.

Maps

Among all the paraphernalia you're taking, no item is more important than a map. For your present purposes you want a United States Geological Survey topographic map, popularly called a "topo." *No map in this book should be considered a substitute for a topo.*

The U.S.G.S. topos pinpoint trails, roads, contours, elevations, drainages, water courses, lakes, meadows, forests, valleys, and man-made additions to the area. The most accurately detailed are the 15-minute maps (minutes of latitude and longitude), which cover a quadrangle of about 13 by 17 miles, usually on a scale of 1 inch to a mile, with a contour interval of 80 feet. Thirty-minute quadrangles are also available. They are good, but their smaller scale means everything is more compressed.

With one or more of these in hand, you should be able to compare it with the terrain around you and know roughly where you are. Forks in the trail become less confusing, campsites become specific--rather than haphazard--goals. A topo map is absolutely essential.

You can order topographic maps directly from the United States Geological Survey, Distribution Center, in Denver, Colorado 80225. Fifteen-minute quads sell for 75¢, the full park maps for $1.50. If you are unsure about what maps you will need, write to U.S.G.S. for a free index to topographic maps of Wyoming. In addition, they publish a free booklet that will instruct you in the mysteries of interpreting topographic maps. You can also purchase U.S.G.S. topographic maps at park visitor centers and at local outdoor equipment stores.

The U.S.G.S. 15-minute quads are reliable but not infallible. Don't be upset if what appears on the map doesn't match what is in front of you. You will still have to use common sense.

Cameras

In high mountain country there are sharp lighting contrasts. Forests are full of shadows. Use a light meter, preferably one that measures spot as well as average readings. Snow and ice will fool your meter into giving readings that are wrong for your subject. Open the diaphragm 2 stops more than the meter indicates in order to compensate for glare. Above timberline there is so much sky that the extra light will confuse your meter. For more realistic readings, aim the meter more toward the ground than you normally would. If your camera has a through-the-lens meter, that device will do the job, but it lacks the flexibility—and probably the accuracy—of a separate meter. When you depend on an attached meter, you stand a better chance of getting the photo you want if you bracket the shot with several exposures.

You won't need filters for color film. It's always worthwhile to keep a skylight filter over your lens to protect it against scratches. Use a medium yellow filter if you're shooting black and white.

In this sort of country, a wide-angle lens is generally the most useful, particularly in the vicinity of the high peaks and deep canyons. New panoramas present themselves every time you look in another direction. For a 35mm camera, a 28mm or even a 21mm lens is advisable. A 35mm lens doesn't expand the scope of your camera much more than its standard 50mm.

Ninety mm or 135mm telephoto lenses rank next in terms of usefulness. Great for capturing details of the scenic wonders around you. A 200mm lens will certainly help, but without a tripod you need a pretty steady hand, or a shoulder brace. A conveniently positioned rock with a fairly level surface will also do, but don't count on one always being where you want it. Any lens with a focal length longer than 200mm definitely requires a tripod, and probably a cable release. (Strictly for serious wildlife photographers. The opportunities are sensational *if* you're willing to lug the extra weight.)

Nature buffs interested in closeups of wildflowers and butterflies might also consider macro lenses. Particularly those with a focal length longer than 50mm.

There are even some situations where the normal 50mm lens that came with your camera is the most suitable. For almost every occasion on this backpacking excursion, you will be well prepared if you take along a wide-angle, a normal, and a medium telephoto. If 3 is too many, take a wide-angle and a telephoto.

For the camera buff there is no such thing as too much film. Allow at least a roll a day. It takes a lot of shooting— even for professionals—to come up with a few really superb pictures.

The abundance of lighting variables raises questions about what kind of color film to take. A medium speed film should handle most situations you're likely to encounter. It gives you more latitude in dark forests and handles all lighting with more color warmth than high-speed film.

Fishing

The pristine waters of Yellowstone and Grand Teton—lakes, rivers, streams, ponds, brooks—offer some of the most spectacular trout fishing in the American West. Sport species include cutthroat (named for the red mark on its jaw), rainbow, brown, brook, and lake (also called mackinaw) trout, Arctic grayling, and mountain whitefish. Only the cutthroat trout, grayling, and whitefish are natives.

A policy of artificial stocking has been abandoned, but the damage has been done. To a person whose primary interest is the quality of the fishing—it is terrific—"damage" may seem like a peculiar word; and the question of native versus introduced species may appear to be over-concern with ecological esthetics. But, if a wilderness is to remain truly wild, it must be maintained in its original state with minimal meddling by man. Native fish that were interesting in their own right, both as battlers and as food, are fewer. Their decline has forced the adoption of stringent regulations on park fishing so that what remains may be preserved. There may be many cutthroat trout, but they are not there simply for humans to consume. Numerous other creatures—the grizzly, otter, mink, pelican, osprey, kingfisher, heron, and others—all prey on this fish: It is a vital link in the ecosystem. It has been estimated that pelicans alone—most of them from the Molly Islands colony—

consume up to *400,000* cutthroat each year.

You can pick up a copy of fishing regulations at visitor centers or ranger stations. They will tell you where and how you can fish, and which fish you can keep. Generally, fishing with bait is prohibited. In some streams, only fly-fishing is permitted. That's because you must not keep (and eat) depleted "wild" fish like the grayling; and studies show that about 48 percent of all fish which are caught on bait and then released eventually die. For those hooked on lures and flies the death rate goes down to about 4 percent after release.

Because of increased fishing in the backcountry, park officials are initiating the policy of "catch and release." You can still have your fun, if not a meal. To do so, remove barbs from the hooks on your lures and flies. When you catch a fish, unhook it carefully so you don't tear its mouth and drop it back into the water. Make sure you wet your hands before you touch the fish. Dry hands may cause a fungus that could wind up killing it anyway.

You must obtain a permit to fish anywhere in the park. You may obtain a permit and current regulations from any visitor center or ranger station in the park.

Safety

The wilderness naturally presents some hazards, but traveling through the backcountry is not a perilous venture—if you use your head. To a large extent, safety is common sense and logic.

Before You Go

Stop at the park ranger station before you take off into the wilderness. The rangers there will issue you a backcountry use permit (no charge). Permits have become necessary as more and more people are attracted to the wilderness. Such a system might seem overly restrictive at first, but it is necessary to prevent overuse and overcrowding in the backcountry. Without it, much wilderness would be destroyed. It's for your own benefit.

It's also for your safety. When you obtain permits for a series of campsites you are, in effect, filing an itinerary. Park personnel are then aware of your whereabouts should an emergency develop. Be sure to follow your planned itinerary as closely as possible.

Before leaving, discuss your trip plans with one of the rangers. He'll fill you in on current conditions, warn you away from areas that are, at that moment, dangerous or otherwise unappealing, and supply you with a variety of helpful tips. Aside from your traveling companions, the park rangers are the best friends you have in the wilderness.

The ranger will also provide you with a pamphlet containing backcountry rules and regulations. They are the outgrowth of decades of park management and all of them arc designed to protect both you and the park. Don't flout them—violators will be fined by a United States Magistrate.

There may be a few other items of special business between you and the rangers. If canoeing or boating is on your agenda, you'll need a boat permit. Fishermen should also obtain a permit and a copy of the backcountry fishing regulations. The use of firearms is prohibited on most parklands.

The Park Service has designated a set number of backcountry campsites and permits are issued only for those locations. With few exceptions, they arc issued on a first-come, first-served basis. If the sites in an area are filled for a particular night, no more permits are given out.

Brief junkets are a good alternative if there are no permits left for the area you want to explore on the day you would like to leave. Even though your primary goal may be a deep penetration of the interior, short hikes act as a sort of decompression chamber from the "civilization" you've left behind. If, like most people, you are an urban dweller, you probably screen out much of the world around you. Some short hiking can help you slow down, open your lungs, tune up your deadened sensitivity, and make you aware of the sights and scents and textures of the natural universe. A day trip or 2 helps you to get the "feel" of the land, work up to the big plunge.

Don't wait until you're half way up a mountain to open your map. You should familiarize yourself with it and the trail descriptions in this book before you leave.

You are going to find that distances shown on the map are no indication of how long it will take to get from point A to point B. You will also find that climbing steep trails above 7,000 feet with a heavy pack on your back is a slower process than you had imagined. Don't exhaust yourself by trying to travel too far or too fast. Backpacking is a *leisure* activity. A slow, steady, measured pace is preferable to short bursts of speed followed by long rests. Rest when you feel the need, but try not to dally more than 10 minutes each time. Lunchtime should be your long break.

After You Get Lost

Trails in Yellowstone are for the most part, well-marked (unlike trails in some nearby national forests). Look for bright orange squares of metal nailed to the trees at regular intervals. These markers are always helpful, but on snow-covered trails and meadows where the grass is over your head, they are indispensable. In many backcountry meadows, there are tall poles to mark the route.

A reasonably good system of trail signs indicates routes and distances. They can be helpful, but it is never wise to depend solely on those signs for directions. That's why you have a topo map and a compass.

Do *not* leave designated trails unless you're a *very experienced hiker*. Cross-country travel can be rewarding, but only if you know what you're doing. Even if you do, you *must* be given permission to travel off established trails, and the use permit you carry must indicate those plans.

Almost any trail can become difficult to follow at times. If it does, stop to consider the rate of climb or descent that it has been following. Most trails are pretty consistent. Yours will almost certainly continue at the same up or down rate that it has been maintaining. To relocate it, move along the same contour you were following without making any major changes in your elevation.

Vegetation may be hiding the trail. Push the underbrush aside and check for human and animal tracks on the ground. If you can't find it nearby, look for a post on the horizon. Other signs to watch for are wooden poles or metal fenceposts on hillsides, branches and willow limbs sawed or cut from trees, and excavated stream crossings.

When you reach an unmarked trail junction, take the fork that most closely follows the grade and general direction of the trail you've been following. If you're still doubtful, hunt for footprints. You want the fork that shows the most signs of human traffic, not animals. Most unmarked junctions occur at points where hiking paths are intersected by outfitter and game trails. The latter can be identified by the fact that they follow much steeper grades, and the route tends to be a straight line rather than one which moves along contours. Because such trails may be heavily traveled by horses and other animals, they can give you the idea that they are the most used and, therefore, the most desirable to follow. Don't be misled. Search for signs of other hikers and follow them.

Any one of the above strategies should have you back on the proper trail within a quarter-mile or so.

If you do get to a point where you find yourself saying, "I am lost, hopelessly lost," the first thing to do is: do nothing. Sit down. Reconnoiter. Reconstruct your previous movements on the topo map and find your general location. The solution to your problem will probably become obvious. In any case, don't rush around frantically—you will get more lost, if that's possible. Plan first, then act.

Look for water. Small streams eventually flow into larger ones which parallel trails or roads. All major drainages eventually lead back to civilization.

Remember, also, that trails were laid out with a reasonable amount of logic. Though there are many acres in the parks, there are many trails criss-crossing them.

Watching Your Step

There are certain areas and certain times that require extra caution. Be wary of loose rock. Never travel at night or in a blinding storm. When a storm pounces and lightning is suddenly striking nearby peaks, try to leave the area. If you get caught above timberline, avoid exposed ledges or caves. Keep low and remove metal objects, such as your pack and climbing hardware. Use your boot soles as insulation between you and the ground—squat, don't sit.

Backcountry trails frequently ford fairly large streams. Often the current is swift. It's treacherous early in the season when the waterways are swollen by melting snow. The rocks are slippery. Keep shoes on when you're crossing, but remove your socks. Wet socks can cause blisters. If you can find a fallen branch nearby, it could be helpful as a supporting staff. Unfasten the waist strap of your pack to give yourself freedom of movement should you fall. Feel your way across with great deliberation. Keep your eyes on the opposite bank and move slowly. Don't lift your feet. Your balance becomes shakier and the current can upend you.

In Yellowstone the thermal areas can be a hazard. The Park Service has erected boardwalks and placed warning signs around boiling hot springs in heavily visited areas. There is no such protection in the backcountry. The ground around these areas is often only a thin crust. It can easily crack open under your weight. More than one unwary wild animal has been parboiled this way. (You can see their remains around Skeleton Pool.)

Blisters and Burns

Blisters are the most common complaint requiring first aid on a hike. The possibility of developing them can be minimized if you do a thorough job of breaking in your shoes before you begin. At the *first* sign of rubbing or tenderness, place some molefoam over the sore areas. If you wait too long, a blister will form. If one does develop, don't apply the molefoam directly over it. Cut a hole in the molefoam to fit the size and shape of the blister and place it around the area. At the end of the day, check the amount of fluid in the blister. If there's a lot, sterilize a needle with a match, prick the blister and drain it. Cover it with a band-aid.

Ticks can be a problem on early summer hikes. Take the time to thoroughly check for them on your body each night in camp. If you find one imbedded in your skin, a little alcohol applied to the spot should send him packing. When there is no alcohol handy, a steady hand holding a burning match near the spot serves the same purpose.

Sunburn can be a problem at high altitudes. Apply suntan lotion or glacier cream (near snow and ice) frequently. Use sun screen if you're particularly susceptible. A wide-brimmed hat will protect your nose and ears.

Your first aid kit should include:

- Molefoam or moleskin.
- Needle.
- Band-aids (large, medium, small).
- Alcohol (optional).

Obviously that won't take care of serious injuries, but for the commonplace, you have everything else you need in your pack. Clean handkerchiefs or bandannas can serve as bandages. Soap cleans minor wounds. Water purification tablets aren't necessary in this wilderness.

Grinning Down Bears

One of the best reasons for trekking through the wilderness is to see the wildlife, yet animals are one of the main reasons more people don't go. The wild beasts that roam here should not be feared so much as they should be respected. Know their capabilities and their habits. Be prepared.

Respect is one key word in your relationship with wild animals; distance is another. That applies even to the smaller creatures. It may seem perfectly innocuous to feed a seed to a little chipmunk, until he nips you. Next thing you know, you've got a case of tularemia or rabies.

But it is not chipmunks that strike fear into the heart. It is bears. Black bears and grizzly bears.

Hopefully, you know enough to steer clear of unattended cubs. They may appear cuddly, but their mother is nearby, and she will not tolerate your interest in her offspring. The thing most likely to bring you trouble from bears is food in your camp. Bears have an extraordinary sense of smell. Normally, packaged dried foods don't cause a problem. Where fires are permitted, burn leftover scraps from all meals. Burn empty food containers to remove lingering odors. Never leave any food unattended around camp. After you have a clean camp, place all other food supplies in your pack and tote it about 50 yards away from your campsite. Hoist it up into a tree for the night.

After years of contact with humans, many black bears have lost all fear of man. Should one invite himself to dinner, it's best not to argue. The bear wants your food, not you. Sometimes a lot of hollering and banging will frighten him away; sometimes it won't. Black bears are not in the same league with grizzlies, but they can swing a mean paw. If you meet one on the trail, chances are he will run from you.

To avoid grizzlies, a few extra precautions are in order. Never camp in an area where you have observed one or his fresh signature: droppings (similar in appearance to the human variety), diggings, or tracks (a large paw print with long, pointed clawmarks). If you spot a bear while hiking, make a wide detour around him. Grizzlies are another excellent reason for not traveling at night. The chances of surprising one are much greater after dark. One of the worst things you can do is surprise a grizzly, especially a sow with cubs. If you have reason to believe one is nearby, attach some bells to your pack. Or talk a lot. Announce your presence, because the normal bear really has no desire to meet you and will make his own detour. If your itinerary includes known grizzly country, it's best to travel in groups of 4 or more. Grizzlies are loners. They do not travel in packs, thirsting for human flesh. About the only time they get together is for mating.

Suppose you've taken all the precautions and, one dark day, you round a bend in the trail and find yourself face to face with a grizzly bear. Don't run. It will trigger his natural instinct to pursue, and you cannot outrun him. He can clip along at 30 miles per hour. Walk to the nearest tree with as much calm as you can muster and climb it. Try to get at least 12 feet up. Grizzlies have trouble climbing trees. Black bears don't. Throw down your pack or another object that might distract and delay him while you head for the tree. (It might even short-circuit his interest in you altogether.) If for some reason you must run, head downhill. Grizzlies have a hard time in that direction. Uphill, they can catch you easily.

If you're caught in a spot where there are no trees you should "play dead." Lie down on the ground and curl up with your knees tucked against your chest, hands behind you head and neck (and pray). The grizzly may do nothing more than sniff you, satisfy his curiosity, and depart in peace. Clearly, this sort of strategy will require more guts than you ever thought you had. People have survived encounters with grizzlies by adopting the play dead routine. It does work.

Realistically, just how much danger do grizzlies pose to a backpacker? If you meet one, a lot of danger. But the chances are extremely low. There are no more than 250 in Yellowstone and a handful in the Teton Wilderness just below Yellowstone's southern border. (They were airlifted there by the Park Service because they had a way of camping at designated campsites.) There have been reports of grizzly tracks in Grand Teton National Park but, thus far, only in wilderness areas that have no trails. In this century, 6 people have been killed by grizzlies in *all* North American national parks. The fact of the matter is that if you have seen a big beautiful grizzly—the largest surviving mammal on the continent—you are very fortunate, indeed.

A noisy hiker who keeps a clean, odor-free camp is not likely to have bear problems in the backcountry. All the cautionary measures mentioned here come endorsed and tested, but there are no guarantees. One of the things that makes a grizzly dangerous is his unpredictability. At the ranger station you can get a brochure titled "In Grizzly Country." It discusses bear precautions in more detail.

The most dangerous animal you are actually liable to meet is a moose. They are powerful and speedy; they have nasty dispositions, and depending on the time of year, they can be very aggressive. If a moose is headed your way, give him the right of way. Any moose lying down in your path should be given a wide berth. The time to be watchful is midmorning to late afternoon. Be especially wary during the rutting season (early fall) or any time you are in the vicinity of females with calves. Should a moose charge you, run, but don't attempt to outrun him over a level stretch. Climb a tree, or get behind a big rock or a fallen tree.

Elk and bison tend to move away when you approach. Don't try to get too close, particularly if they have young with them. Another time to be on your toes is the elk rutting season in early fall. The male, crazed with lust, is in no mood to trifle with you.

There are so few wolves and mountain lions in the region you would need a lot of luck to see one. You will probably see coyotes, but they will run from you. Tales of attacks on humans by any of these predators are popular mythology. Verified reports are virtually nonexistent.

Don't feed or pester any park animals, from bears to chipmunks. Not just because they might bite, but because they become dependent on these handouts. Come winter the tourists disappear and many animals starve because they have forgotten how to fend for themselves. Respect the animals. Keep your distance.

Backcountry Etiquette

One of the things you must bring with you is your manners. There was a time when wilderness explorers could be casual about matters like garbage and campfires. That time is past. More and more people are crowding into the backcountry. A few thoughtless ones can spoil it for everyone. The wilderness is fragile.

When you are looking for a campsite, find a *naturally* level spot for your sleeping bag and tent. There's no need to shovel or flatten earth. Don't dig a trench around your tent. The scars you leave would take years to heal. Beavers are the only engineers allowed to practice here.

No one relishes the idea of drinking somebody else's bathwater. Remember that when you are washing yourself, your kitchen utensils, or anything else. Don't use soap directly in any of the lakes, pools, streams, or other natural running waters. Don't rinse anything in them. Fill a cookpot with water and carry it away from the stream to do all your bathing and camp clean-up. Make sure you tote it some distance away from the stream so that when you empty the dirty water it doesn't drain back. Be not a polluter of wild waters.

In Yellowstone, it is strictly forbidden to swim or bathe in any of the natural hot springs or pools—no matter what the temperature of the water may be.

If you're camping in an area where fires are allowed, use a spot already scarred by previous fires. Build your fire in an open space, never under a canopy of trees. You should not use boulders or large rocks as backdrops for your hearth—that will blacken them forever. Keep your fire clear of exposed tree roots. Remember, the only fuel you're permitted is wood that has already fallen. Use it with discretion. The next party will want a fire too. Put out the fire before you retire. When you leave camp, be absolutely certain that your fire is dead out. If the ashes are still warm, wet them down.

A toilet is the only thing you are allowed to dig in the wilderness and, if you do it right, nobody should know but you. Nature's own disposal system is at your service. Biological action within the top 6 to 8 inches of soil decomposes organic materials.

Carry out all garbage; cans, bottles, plastics, aluminum foil, etc. Burying won't do. Eventually your trash will be unearthed by sharp-nosed animals, or frost action, and the campsite will turn into a garbage dump. Flatten all cans and drop them into one of the plastic sacks you brought along. The containers you packed in full, will weigh a lot less as you pack them out empty.

Don't shortcut switchbacks. It only accelerates erosion and scars the land forever. Don't discard any cigarettes or matches unless they are 100% out. Field-strip your butts. Smokey the Bear is watching you. Don't roll or throw rocks down mountains or into canyons. Somebody might be down there. Don't toss objects into springs, pools, or vents. Don't pick the wildflowers. Don't collect souvenirs. All the above are subject to fines.

Pack animals have the right of way on trails. (If you are planning a backcountry trip by horseback, write in advance to the Chief Ranger's Office in the park. Ask for a copy of current regulations and a list of campsites approved for horse parties.)

You are not allowed to operate motorized vehicles on the trails or in any area of the park that isn't a proper roadway or parking area. Nor can you ride a bicycle on the hiking trails. (There are several designated bicycle trails in the Old Faithful area. Check with the Old Faithful Visitor Center for exact locations.)

No dogs, cats, or pet monkeys allowed on any trail in the parks, not even if you have them on a leash. Bears and other native beasts do not like domestic pets. And it's *their* park.

Trail Descriptions

by Orville Bach

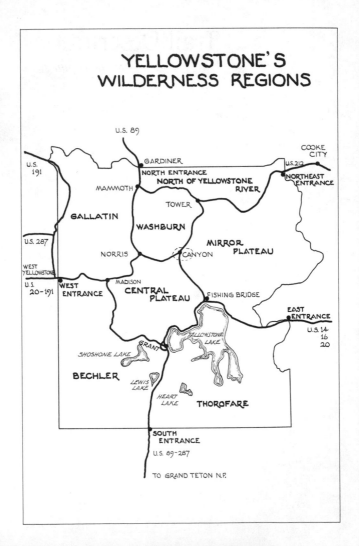

YELLOWSTONE'S
WILDERNESS REGIONS

U.S. 89

COOKE CITY

GARDINER

U.S. 191

U.S. 212

NORTH ENTRANCE

NORTHEAST ENTRANCE

MAMMOTH

NORTH OF YELLOWSTONE RIVER

TOWER

GALLATIN

WASHBURN

U.S. 287

MIRROR PLATEAU

NORRIS

CANYON

WEST YELLOWSTONE

U.S. 20-191

WEST ENTRANCE

MADISON

CENTRAL PLATEAU

FISHING BRIDGE

EAST ENTRANCE

U.S. 14 16 20

SHOSHONE LAKE

GRANT

YELLOWSTONE LAKE

BECHLER

LEWIS LAKE

HEART LAKE

THOROFARE

SOUTH ENTRANCE

U.S. 89-287

TO GRAND TETON N.P.

MAP LEGEND

RANGER STATION	☉
LAKE	⬭
RIVER OR CREEK	〰
PARK BOUNDARY	————
PAVED ROAD	▬▬▬▬
ONE WAY ROAD	—→——→——→
TRAIL	– – – – – –
SPRING	♀
WATERFALL	⌇
CONTINENTAL DIVIDE	••••••••••••••••••
MOUNTAIN SUMMIT	• 10,336
PATROL CABIN	▪
PASS	⇌

This legend is the key for all maps that follow.

Union Falls (250 ft.)

Bechler Region

The Bechler area or Cascade Corner of Yellowstone National Park is truly magnificent; no other region in the park better exemplifies Yellowstone's more gentle and serene wilderness. It is known appropriately as "waterfalls country"—21 of the park's 41 waterfalls are located here in the southwest corner of the park. They are found primarily along the principal streams of the Bechler area—the Bechler and Falls rivers, and the Boundary and Mountain Ash creeks, all tributaries of Snake River—and many are over 100 ft. high.

Besides the waterfalls, several other attractions draw backpackers to the Bechler's 100 mi. or more of trails. Because of the lower altitude and warmer, moister climate, the area contains rich vegetation and an abundant supply of surface water. The forests include large spruce and fir, and tall white-barked aspen. Undergrowth includes raspberry, thimbleberry, and huckleberry bushes, along with the various ferns and mosses. The Bechler Meadows, with the majestic Teton Range behind it to the south, is one of the largest and more beautiful meadows in the park.

Important wildlife species frequently sighted here include moose, wapiti, deer, trumpeter swan, and sandhill crane. In addition, this area sports some of the best fishing waters in Yellowstone Park. Remarkably large cutthroat trout are often caught from the Bechler River.

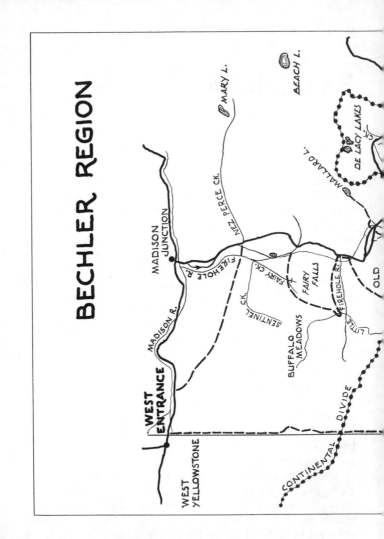

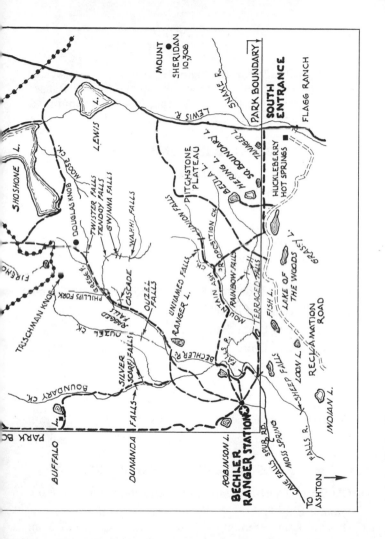

The trailheads for the majority of hikes in the Bechler region lie in the immediate vicinity of the Bechler Ranger Station, 25 mi. northeast of Ashton, Idaho, on a spur road leading eastward from U.S. Highway 191.

BECHLER REGION TRAILS

Bechler Ranger Station to Three River Junction .. 13.5 mi.

South Boundary Trail
(Bechler Ranger Station to South Entrance) ..... 20 mi.

West Boundary Trail
(Bechler Ranger Station to West Yellowstone) .... 36 mi.

Bechler Ranger Station to Buffalo Lake .... 15 mi.

Bechler River Trail
(Kepler Cascades to Three River Junction) ..... 15.5 mi.

Cave Falls to Union Falls .... 11.5 mi.

Grassy Lake to Union Falls .... 7 mi.

Grassy Lake to Beula Lake .... 2.5 mi.

Pitchstone Plateau Trail .... 18.5 mi.

Divide Lookout Trail .... 1.7 mi.

Shoshone Lake Trail
(South Entrance Road to Bechler River Trail) ... 16.5 mi.

Shoshone Lake to Lewis Lake (Canoe Trip) ...... 13 mi.

TRAILS FROM OLD FAITHFUL AREA

Old Faithful Visitor Center to Observation Point ..0.8 mi.

Summit Lake Trail
(Biscuit Basin to Summit Lake) .... 7.5 mi.

Mystic Falls Trail
(Biscuit Basin to Mystic Falls) . . . . 0.9 mi.

Fairy Creek Trail
(Biscuit Basin to Fairy Creek) . . . . 13 mi.

Fairy Falls-Imperial Geyser Trail . . . . 3.1 mi.

Fern Cascades Loop Trail . . . . 3 mi.

Mallard Lake Trail
(Old Faithful to Mallard Lake) . . . . 3.5 mi.

Old Fountain Pack Trail
(Lower Geyser Basin to West Entrance Road) . 13 mi.

BECHLER REGION TRAILS

Bechler Ranger Station to Three River Junction (13.5 mi.)

From the Bechler Ranger Station (where a ranger is stationed throughout the summer months), this trail winds 3.5
mi. through dense forest before reaching the Bechler Meadows at Boundary Creek. The dominant tree here, as
throughout the park, is the lodgepole pine. Although 80
percent of the park is forested, there are relatively few
species of trees; almost all are conifers, and three-quarters
of these are lodgepole pine. The lodgepole can grow to an
elevation of between 7,000 and 8,500 ft., although the
Bechler area is somewhat lower (approx. 6,400 ft.). For this
reason the plant growth in this forest is much more dense
and varied than in other lodgepole forests at higher elevations throughout the park. You will notice numbers of dead
trees and branches scattered on the forest floor. This is
because the lodgepole pine has a very shallow root system
and is unable to withstand strong winds and heavy snows. It

is not a good idea to make camp under a group of dead and swaying lodgepoles on a windy evening.

Approximately 1.5 mi. from the Ranger Station, to the left of the trail, is a small pond framed by aspens. Immediately behind it lies a meadow that is frequently a feeding spot for moose, especially during early morning and late afternoon.

At 3.5 mi. from the Ranger Station the trail emerges from the forest into Bechler Meadows and Boundary Creek campground. Bechler Meadows are home to a variety of birdlife. You can usually see the sandhill crane flying low over the meadows. Many years ago, before the whooping crane reached a tragically low level, sightings were made of that majestic bird. Note that the meadows, being located below the plateaus of the area, receive a great deal of spring runoff and as a result are quite swampy early in the summer. During the height of the spring runoff they are practically inaccessible, so it is best to plan your trip for no earlier than July 1.

As you cross the bridge over Boundary Creek and start over the meadows, Ouzel Falls appears about 4 mi. to the north plunging over the edge of the plateau. This giant 230 ft. waterfall remains impressive throughout the summer, although it is most spectacular when some runoff is still present. Two miles across the meadow lies the Bechler River (named for Gustavus R. Bechler, topographer on the Snake River Division of the Hayden Expedition in 1872). Bechler Ford campground is located here, 5.5 mi. from the Bechler Ranger Station.

A bridge crosses the Bechler River at the campground. Leaving the river, you walk a short distance through trees before emerging into another meadow, the last to be crossed before entering Bechler Canyon, already clearly visible in the distance.

The scenery is superb as the trail winds up the Bechler Canyon. The forest consists of spruce and fir, with an assortment of ferns and mosses, and innumerable huckleberry bushes. Shortly after entering the canyon, a rockslide area extends all the way down into the river. For 0.25 mi. the trail is difficult to travel. Horse parties must ford the river and go around this area. In the heart of Bechler Canyon lies Colonnade Falls, a terraced waterfall consisting of 2 plunges of the Bechler River totaling 102 ft. Upstream 0.3 mi. from Colonnade lies Iris Falls, similar to Colonnade Falls in appearance but dropping only 45 ft. Once past Iris Falls, the trail continues to climb steadily up the canyon, with many small falls and cascades along the way. Between Iris Falls and Three River Junction it crosses the Bechler River no less than 3 times. Some fords are waist-deep all summer long. A backpacker would definitely have problems crossing them before July. About 1 mi. southwest of Three River Junction campground, to the right of the trail, is a very steep cascade. Although less than 0.2 mi. from the trail, it is located in dense forest, but it is worth a side trip as it is at least 200 ft. high. Three River Junction campground lies in a flat, open area surrounded to the north and south by steep canyon walls. The increased use of this area, particularly by large horse parties, has resulted in a ranger being stationed here throughout the summer.

There are numerous hot pools and springs at Three River Junction, causing both hot and cold streams. (In some pools, color is produced when water absorbs the red rays from sunlight and reflects blue. Often this combines with yellow-red shades of mineral deposits and algal growths to produce emerald greens. The temperature of the pool itself may help determine the color, as different forms of algae thrive at different temperature levels.)

At the foot of the canyon walls on both sides of the campground the scattered rocks and boulders are covered by yellow-bellied marmot (also called groundhogs, woodchucks, or roundchucks).

The actual junction of the 3 rivers is about 0.5 mi. upstream from the campground. Here the Phillips, Gregg, and Ferris forks unite to form the Bechler River. As the trail crosses the Ferris Fork, Three River Junction lies just off to the left (N); to the right (S) on the Ferris Fork is Ragged Falls, a 50 ft. drop. Although there is no maintained trail along the Ferris Fork, there are interesting sights and the traveling is not too difficult. (However, any travel away from established trails should be by experienced hikers only, and permission must be received when obtaining your backcountry use permit.) Approximately 200 yds. after crossing the Ferris Fork, you will come to an open space that is diagonally crossed by another trail. This trail bends down to the Gregg Fork, where it terminates. It is apparently "maintained" by wildlife and is the best route to explore the Ferris Fork. (It will lead you past a hot pool that ranks with the best in the park.)

As you continue up the Ferris Fork, 4 waterfalls appear within a relatively short distance of each other. The first, Tendoy Falls, is the most impressive, located 0.9 mi. upstream from Ragged Falls, a 45 ft. sheer drop into a large pool. Half a mile upstream from Tendoy is Gwinna Falls, a 20 ft. drop. Another 0.5 mi. brings you to Sluiceway Falls (35 ft.). Only 0.2 mi. upstream from Sluiceway is Wahhi Falls, a sharp 50 ft. plunge of the Ferris Fork. From Wahhi

Falls the slopes of Pitchstone Plateau are clearly visible to the south and east.

South Boundary Trail
(Bechler Ranger Station to South Entrance) (20 mi.)

(Note that in order to travel safely in this particular area, it will be necessary to order from U.S.G.S. a 15-min. topo map of Grassy Lake, Wyoming, 1956. Maps of the Yellowstone area may be ordered from U.S.G.S., Distribution Section, in Denver, Colorado.)

The South Boundary Trail is not recommended in its entirety, since the park's boundary trails were designed more for border patrol purposes than for scenic hiking. However, there are some portions of this trail, especially in the vicinity of the Falls River, that are beautiful. Trailheads for this hike are the Bechler Ranger Station and the South Entrance; access to this trail is also possible from several other spur trails which cross it.

If you choose to begin from the Bechler Station, it is important to keep in mind that you must ford the Falls River after 2 mi. The river here is quite wide and for most of the summer will definitely present a problem to the backpacker, so you may want to consider joining the trail at some point farther east. The more beautiful sections occur where it touches on the Falls River just north of Winegar Lake (4.5 mi. from Bechler Station). From this point until it crosses Calf Creek 2 mi. upstream, the scenery is superb. At only 6,450 ft. the forest contains spruce, fir, and aspen, in addition to lodgepole pine, and the vegetation is quite rich. The fishing for rainbow and Snake River cutthroat trout in the Falls River along this stretch is excellent,

and chances of spotting moose are very good. After crossing
Calf Creek, the trail climbs 800 ft. through timber to join
the Reclamation Road at the 8.5 mi. mark. (If you cannot
ford the river, you can reach this area by beginning from
Calf Creek.) From Grassy Lake to the South Entrance, the
trail follows the park boundary for most of the way. At
14.5 mi. (from Bechler Station), the Beula Lake Trail is
crossed. The lake is now only 2 mi. away. At 16 mi. the
trail passes South Boundary Lake, which reportedly contains a population of small cutthroat. From here it is 4
more miles to the South Entrance.

West Boundary Trail
(Bechler Ranger Station to West Yellowstone)   (36 mi.)

The West Boundary Trail from Bechler Station to West Yellowstone is not recommended because the land is dry and
the scenery monotonous. This trail is used by park rangers
for border patrols, primarily to ensure that hunters respect
the park boundary.

The first 2 mi. take you to Robinson Lake, which is
surrounded by meadows. Birdlife is abundant here, and
chances are good for spotting moose and elk. Rock Creek,
which rises from Robinson Lake, contains only small populations of pan-sized cutthroat and rainbow. Beyond this
lake, the attractions on the West Boundary Trail become
few and far between.

X Bechler Ranger Station to Buffalo Lake   (15 mi.)

This trail takes you through interesting wilderness scenery
past one of the park's most beautiful waterfalls. The first
1.4 mi. coincide with the Bechler Ranger Station-Three

River Junction Trail, but at that point our trail forks off to the left. Just beyond this fork, to the left, is a small pond covered with lilypads. It is a watering spot often visited by deer early in the morning. The trail crosses the heart of the Bechler Meadows, affording fine views of the surrounding country and of the plateaus to the north and east.

After crossing Bechler Meadows, the trail enters a forest (chiefly lodgepole) but continues along many open areas and meadows providing fine views and opportunities for wildlife sightings. Blue and ruffed grouse are frequently observed here.

During the last 4 mi. to Dunanda Falls, there is only 1 cold stream from which to drink at the 6.5 mi. mark. (All other streams are warm, due to nearby thermal activity.) Another mile brings you to Silver Scarf Falls, not a sheer drop, but a sloping cascade of some 250 ft. Continuing across a hill the trail passes above the brink of Dunanda Falls on the east and affords a breath-taking view. However, the most spectacular and satisfying view of the 150 ft. drop of the Boundary Creek is from the foot of the falls. A steep grassy slope from the trail permits easy access to this area. There are hot pools along the stream below the falls which contain algae.

There are not very many travelers beyond Dunanda Falls, although the wilderness scenery to Buffalo Lake is very beautiful. The trail continues 2.5 mi. before crossing Boundary Creek, and emerging into a meadow with a steep canyon wall rising to the east. The wall is actually the edge of the Madison Plateau, and its continuation can be seen to the north for quite some distance. Buffalo Lake is reached at 15 mi. Meadows extend away from the northern and southwestern shores of the lake (favorite feeding spots for elk, moose, and deer, especially in early morning and late afternoon). There are no fish in Buffalo Lake, but its shores are home to numerous species of birds; chances of spotting trumpeter swan and sandhill crane here are excellent. Beyond Buffalo Lake the trail continues for 1 mi. before it joins the West Boundary Trail, which parallels the park boundary.

Bechler River Trail
(Kepler Cascades to Three River Junction)   (15.5 mi.)

A complete trip across the Bechler country from Bechler Ranger Station to Kepler Cascades is an excellent way to see the area, but trail connections are something of a problem. For this reason, the trail description begins at Kepler Cascades and ends at Three River Junction. The trailhead for this trip is located near Kepler Cascades, a 2.7 mi. drive southeast from Old Faithful overpass (toward Grant) on the Grand Loop Road. (There is a small parking lot at the cascades where you may leave your car.) The Kepler Cascades are a series of small falls on the Firehole River totaling about 125 ft. amid canyon walls. A boardwalk leading to an overlook provides a fine view. The trail to Lone Star Geyser and points beyond begins about 100 yds. up the road from Kepler Cascades. You can also reach Lone Star Geyser by beginning from Old Faithful Ranger Station, but it is approximately 1 mi. longer, and the trail closely parallels the Grand Loop Road part of the way. For the first 2.5 mi. from Kepler Cascades to Lone Star Geyser you will actually be following the old Lone Star Geyser spur road, which was converted in 1972 to a foot and bicycle trail only.

The Firehole River is closed to fishing from Old Faithful up to the footbridge that is beyond Lone Star Geyser since it supplies the Old Faithful area with drinking water. As you follow the old spur road along the river, you will pass by the mouth of Spring Creek at 1.6 mi. Watch for wildflowers here, especially harebell and Indian paintbrush. At the 2 mi. mark you will pass by a meadow through which the Firehole winds. This is a good spot to look for elk, particularly in early morning and late afternoon.

Lone Star Geyser is a geyserite cone 10 to 12 ft. high. Eruptions occur every 3 hrs. or so, lasting for about 25 min. Minor eruptions begin 1 hr. before the main eruption.

It is important to keep on the established trail in this area, as there are a number of potentially dangerous thermal features. If Lone Star Geyser is the primary objective of your hike, you may want to make a loop trip back, following the 3.8 mi. long trail to Old Faithful Ranger Station.

Continuing south from Lone Star Geyser, the trail passes through dense lodgepole for 0.5 mi. before meeting the bridge crossing of the Firehole. The Firehole was named by early trappers who found a burnt-over forested valley, or "hole," through which the water coursed. Jim Bridger, legendary scout, fur trapper, and mountainman, told tales of how he was able to catch a trout in this stream and cook it in a boiling pool without ever leaving his place on the riverbank. The warm waters provide excellent dry-fly fishing, weeks ahead of the other park streams. The angler will find early hatches of insects all along the Upper Firehole.

After crossing the Firehole, the trail heads into heavy timber, touching on the river only once more at the 4 mi. mark (from Kepler Cascades, 1 mi. from the bridge). There are several more hot springs in this area. Just upstream the river meanders through a large meadow carpeted with harebell and fringed gentian.

The trail now begins to climb steadily toward Grants Pass through extremely dry timbered land consisting almost exclusively of lodgepole pine. At Grants Pass you will have traveled 6 mi. from the trailhead at Kepler Cascades. The pass itself is quite inconspicuous, marked only by an old sign on a tree. The trail descends 0.4 mi. to the edge of an open area and the junction with the Shoshone Lake Trail, which forks off to the left (SE). From here it is 2 mi. to Shoshone Geyser Basin, and 3 mi. to Shoshone Lake (see *Shoshone Lake Trail*).

For the next 4 mi. the route continues once again through heavy timber, crossing the Continental Divide 3 times before reaching the Littles Fork, at which point you will have traveled 11 mi. from Kepler Cascades. When you finally emerge from the forest at Littles Fork, Douglas Knob appears directly in front of you a little less than 1 mi. away. (Trischman Knob looms 2 mi. in the distance to the northwest, but you cannot see it unless you walk up the Littles Fork a short way. These natural features were named after 2 early park rangers who had reputations as extremely rugged mountainmen.)

Less than 1 mi. from Trischman Knob, to the northeast, lies Madison Lake and the Upper Firehole River Valley. The lake is not too difficult to locate, but any travel away from established trails should be by experienced hikers only, and permission must be received when obtaining your backcountry use permit. Madison Lake is a large body of water, but very shallow. The surrounding meadow is quite lush, and the birdlife varied and abundant. This is an excellent spot to look for trumpeter swan, sandhill crane, and various species of duck. It is also a favorite feeding spot for elk, but too far upstream on the Firehole for the trout fishing to be any good.

Madison Lake is the starting point of the Firehole River. The lake was visited by Professor F.H. Bradley of the U.S. Geological Survey, and was appropriately named "Madison" Lake by Bradley, since he realized that it was the ultimate lake source for the Madison River. The Firehole flows from Madison Lake to Madison Junction, at which point the Firehole and Gibbon rivers unite to form the Madison River. (At Three Forks, Montana, Madison, Gallatin, and Jefferson rivers unite to form the mighty Missouri River.)

Twister Falls, which consists of a series of small falls and cascades between perpendicular canyon walls, is reached at the 13 mi. mark. Another 0.5 mi. brings you to the edge of a canyon where you can see the Gregg Fork below and, 0.3 mi. to the north, Tempe Cascade of the Littles Fork, which joins the Gregg Fork at this point.

The trail continues along the Gregg Fork until the Ferris Fork and Ragged Falls come into view on the south side of the trail (15 mi.). Here you cross the Ferris Fork and once again emerge from heavy timber to enter the Three River Junction area. Here the Ferris, Phillips, and Gregg forks unite to form the Bechler River.

✖ Cave Falls to Union Falls (11.5 mi.)

Cave Falls, the starting point for this hike, is located at the end of the spur road that extends into the Bechler country. To get there you have to take a 56 mi. drive south from

West Yellowstone on U.S. 191 to Ashton, Idaho. From Ashton, you drive east on the Cave Falls Road for 25 mi. There is a picnic area and campground near Cave Falls. The impressiveness of Cave Falls is not in its height, but in its width and volume. (The name is derived from a large cave at the base of the falls on the west side of the Falls River.) The fishing is generally excellent below the falls for cutthroat and rainbow trout. The river is quite wide and there are some additional impressive falls and cascades both upstream and downstream.

After 0.25 mi. you reach the point where the Bechler River empties into the Falls River. Here the Falls River bends to the east and disappears from view. The trail continues above the Bechler River for several miles through a dense spruce and fir forest. The vegetation is quite rich, with various ferns and mosses and many berry bushes—primarily huckleberry. Keep a close watch along the riverbanks for moose and deer feeding. After 1 mi. you reach Bechler Falls, a 20 ft. drop. Within the next mile you will notice 2 other trails. Both lead westward to Bechler Ranger Station a short distance away.

At 3.2 mi. you come to Rocky Ford. Here the trail fords the Bechler River and continues eastward to Union Falls. As the name indicates, there is a good solid rockbed on which to ford the river and the water is not very deep. Nevertheless, the going can get quite slippery here, so be very careful. After fording the Bechler River, you will actually be on the old Marysville Road, from Marysville, Idaho, to Jackson Hole, built in the 1880's by the Mormons. The wagon marks are still visible in places, although trees have grown up between the tracks.

From Rocky Ford to Union Falls the trail continues to

wind in and out of forest and meadow. The meadows provide beautiful views, especially of the plateau to the north, and wonderful opportunities for sighting wildlife. You may well be able to spot some deer along this stretch, and possibly moose. Five miles from Rocky Ford (8.2 from Cave Falls), the trail crosses the Mountain Ash Creek, which it will now continue to follow most of the way. After crossing the creek and traveling 1.3 mi., you will come to a trail junction. Here the old Marysville Road forks to the right, and a trail follows it most of the way to Grassy Lake, 5.2 mi. away (see *Grassy Lake to Union Falls*). Walking 0.5 mi. beyond the trail junction, you will see a fairly large (unnamed) stream flowing into the Mountain Ash Creek from the north. If you stand at the junction of these streams facing upstream, you will see Mountain Ash Creek on your right and the unnamed stream on your left. There is a large pool where these streams join, providing good trout fishing. Although not shown on topo maps, there is also a large waterfall approximately 1.4 mi. upstream on this unnamed tributary of Mountain Ash Creek. There is no trail along this stream but the going is fairly easy. Very large spruce and fir overhang the grassy banks. The waterfall is 80 to 100 ft. high, and even greater in width. The stream here is warm due to thermal activity upstream from the falls.

You will be able to hear Union Falls long before you see it. The last 50 yds. of the trail climb to an overlook that provides a spectacular view of these magnificent falls. (Two streams unite at the brink to form the 250 ft. drop, hence the name "Union.") The best view of Union Falls is just downstream from the foot of the falls. A steep grassy slope provides access to this area.

Grassy Lake to Union Falls

(7 mi.)

This route to Union Falls is shorter than the one that starts at the Bechler Ranger Station, but it is not nearly as scenic.

Grassy Lake lies just south of the park boundary line. It is reached via the Reclamation Road, which travels some 45 mi. from just below the park boundary at the South Entrance westward to Marysville, Idaho. The Reclamation Road begins a few miles south of the South Entrance at the turnoff from U.S. 89-287 to Huckleberry Hot Springs Ranch. Grassy Lake is a 10 mi. drive. You should be warned, however, that this is a very primitive dirt road, which may be difficult to travel in wet weather.

The trailhead to Union Falls is at the picnic area on the east side of Grassy Lake dam. The trail runs for the first mile through a marshy area full of willows. This is ideal moose country, and deer are also frequently sighted. After 0.7 mi. you reach the Falls River, where it is necessary to ford the ice-cold water. Though shallow, the current is rather swift and the rocks are slippery, so go carefully. (The river contains fine Snake River cutthroat trout.) Another 0.5 mi. brings you to the junction of the Pitchstone Plateau Trail. If time permits, you may be interested in leaving your pack and venturing away from the trail down the Falls River for 1 or 2 mi. (provided you have the necessary permission). Within these 2 mi. there are many cascades and falls. The first mile takes you past Cascade Acres, a pretty stretch of tumbling white water, which goes to Terraced Falls—a series of 5 falls totaling about 150 ft. A mile downstream from Terraced Falls is Rainbow Falls, a 55 ft. drop where the river is forced through a narrow gorge with a deafening roar. The going is rough from Terraced to Rainbow Falls.

After swinging away from the Falls River, the trail climbs steadily through a typical lodgepole pine forest for 2 mi. before dropping sharply to Proposition Creek. Here you can have a refreshing drink and rest for a while before you start climbing back up the steep trail. However, the hill will not seem so steep when you consider that in the 1880's the Mormons were hauling their wagons over this very terrain. For the most part, the trail follows the old Mormon road from Grassy Lake to the junction of the Cave Falls-Union Falls Trail, and from there to Rocky Ford on the Bechler River. (The wagon tracks are still visible in some places.)

From Proposition Creek it is 0.75 mi. to Mountain Ash Creek, where you join the Cave Falls-Union Falls Trail. And from here it is only 2 mi. to Union Falls.

Grassy Lake to Beula Lake (2.5 mi.)

The trailhead is located at the east end of Grassy Lake on the Reclamation Road south of the park. (For directions on how to locate this road, see *Grassy Lake to Union Falls*.) The Forest Service sign at the trailhead gives the distance as 4 mi.; it is actually only 2.5 mi. The trail may be difficult to follow for the first 0.5 mi., since the U.S.F.S. has not used orange trail markers here. Once the park boundary is crossed, the trail is marked like the other maintained trails in the park. The first 0.5 mi. also requires a 400 ft. climb, ending in a superb view of the full length of Grassy Lake.

The remaining 2 mi. pass through dense lodgepole; the lake itself is completely surrounded by forest. Beula Lake, at 7,377 ft., is the ultimate lake source for the Falls River. It has a large population of cutthroat trout.

Pitchstone Plateau Trail   (18.5 mi.)

The trailhead is on the west side of the South Entrance Road, 8 mi. from the entrance station, and 2 mi. south of Lewis Falls. For those interested in Yellowstone's geology, the trip across the Pitchstone Plateau is highly recommended.

The trail climbs 450 ft. in the first mile, then through lodgepole forest to the campsite (5.5 mi.). At 4.5 mi. it passes Phantom Fumarole. (A fumarole differs from a hot spring only in that there is no surface water.)

Yellowstone's geological history is most apparent from high on the Pitchstone Plateau. You are actually standing on a huge lava flow that oozed across the land almost like a glacier, and then quickly cooled to freeze the flow lines and swirls. Today, these lava flow lines are accentuated by many stands of timber, which have grown up right along their edges. (Seen from the air, much of the Pitchstone Plateau looks like a great glacier.) In exploring the area you will find some rhyolite lava flows that appear to be very recent. The Pitchstone Plateau is like a moonscape; a little geological background makes the area fascinating to explore.

From the high point at 8,715 ft. the trail begins its descent, and at 8,400 ft. (the 11 mi. mark) re-enters the forest. The descent continues to the Falls River at 6,920 ft. Just before crossing the river, the trail intersects the Grassy Lake-Union Falls Trail. At the Falls River you will have come 17 mi. Another mile brings you to the Reclamation Road.

Divide Lookout Trail   (1.7 mi.)

The trail begins at the parking area on the south side of the
Grand Loop Road, 6.7 mi. southeast of the Old Faithful
overpass. It crosses Spring Creek and enters a dense forest,
with lodgepole pine predominating and Douglas fir common. At 0.3 mi. you will pass to the right of an area containing very rich undergrowth, due to abundant moisture in
a small, marshy lakebed. The trail continues through a ma-
ture forest to a lookout tower. At 1.3 mi., Shoshone Lake
becomes visible on the left, but there are no unobstructed
distant views available except from the lookout tower at
the end of the trail. The 60 ft. steel tower will not come
into view until you are within 0.1 mi. of it. Built in 1957, it
is not manned except during emergencies.

You can climb the stairs of the lookout, but a locked
door will prevent you from reaching the outside observation deck. The steps have an angle iron railing on both
sides, but are not recommended for youngsters.

✖ Shoshone Lake Trail
(South Entrance Road to Bechler River Trail)   (16.5 mi.)

The trailhead is located on the west side of South Entrance
Road 7.5 mi. from Grant. The trail begins on an old road
about 0.75 mi. north of Lewis Lake campground, directly
opposite the Heart Lake Trail originating from the other
side of the road. This trail leads 4.5 mi. to the southeast
end of Shoshone Lake, where campsites are located. (This
portion of the trail is also referred to as the Channel Trail.)

At the lake, the trail junctions with the DeLacy Creek Trail to the Old Faithful-Grant Road. (For information on this area, see the *Shoshone Lake-Lewis Lake Canoe Trip*.) From the DeLacy Creek Trail junction the trail bends to the west, crosses the Lewis River near the lake's outlet, then climbs 200 ft. up a forested ridge. There it drops back sharply down to a large meadow through which Moose Creek winds into the lake; watch for wildlife at this point. (You have now traveled 6 mi.) The trail then leaves the general area of Shoshone Lake, crossing another small, forested ridge before descending to Moose Creek at the 7.5 mi. mark. At 10 mi. it passes alongside a fine meadow through which Moose Creek meanders, then re-enters lodgepole forest, climbs 200 ft., and finally descends steeply to the southwest shore of Shoshone Lake. You have traveled 13 mi. and it is only 1.5 mi. to the Shoshone Geyser Basin. Cold Mountain and Fall creeks are crossed along the way.

The Shoshone Geyser Basin, located just over the hill from the lake, is well worth a visit. Hot springs flowing into Shoshone Creek ensure an ideal temperature for swimming. There are several geysers here. Union Geyser—containing the Northern, Center, and Southern cones—is perhaps the most interesting, as all 3 cones erupt simultaneously. Unfortunately, eruptions do not occur at regular intervals. The Center Cone erupts up to 115 ft. Little Giant Geyser erupts about twice a day, and attains a height of up to 50 ft. Other geysers—which go off with regularity—are Minute Man Geyser (20 ft. about every 3 min.), Little Bulger Geyser (10 ft. about every 5 min.), and Shield Geyser (3 to 4 ft. as soon as the basin is filled with water).

From the geyser basin the trail follows Shoshone Creek 2 mi. up to the junction with the Bechler River Trail. At this point you will have traveled 16.5 mi. From here it is 6.5 mi. out to the Grand Loop Road. (A new trail now traverses the north shore of Shoshone Lake, connecting Shoshone Geyser Basin with DeLacy Creek.)

Shoshone Lake to Lewis Lake (Canoe Trip) (13 mi.)

The opportunities for canoeing in Yellowstone are limited. Before entering any of the park's waters, you must register your boat at Yellowstone Lake Ranger Station or Grant Village Ranger Station and obtain a permit for its use; this holds true regardless of the type of boat involved. You will be briefed on such factors as the sudden storms that are a recurring feature of Yellowstone (see *Briefed Boating Regulations*). There are 2 areas where you can enjoy extensive canoeing or rafting: Yellowstone Lake, with its Flat Mountain, South and Southeast arms, and the Shoshone Lake-Lewis River-Lewis Lake area. (Yellowstone Lake boating and canoeing is covered under *Canoeing on Yellowstone Lake.*)

There are a number of ways to approach this area. Some people prefer to launch their craft on Lewis Lake and paddle upstream on the Lewis River to Shoshone Lake, returning the same way. Paddling upstream is not too difficult, as the river's current along this stretch is quite slow. For most people with heavy equipment, this is the best approach. However, if your craft is relatively light and easy to carry, and you can make the transportation connection, then the ideal trip is to begin at DeLacy Park, hike in 3.1 mi. to the north shore of Shoshone Lake, and canoe on through to Lewis Lake. A description of this trip follows. The information contained in it will also prove useful if you choose to begin at Lewis Lake rather than Shoshone Lake.

DeLacy Creek trailhead is on the Old Faithful-Grant Road where DeLacy Creek crosses the road, 7.9 mi. from Old Faithful. It is a 3.1 mi. hike from the trailhead to the shore of Shoshone Lake. The first mile of the trail follows DeLacy Creek for the most part through a lodgepole pine forest, before emerging into a meadow. In the last 2 mi. to the lake are fine views of the meadow through which De-Lacy Creek flows. Chances of spotting moose in this area are excellent. The trail continues to follow the meadow's edge to the northernmost shore of Shoshone Lake.

Shoshone Lake was originally named DeLacy Lake for Walter W. DeLacy, an engineer who passed through the Yellowstone region in 1863 in search of gold. However, the Hayden Expedition of 1871 renamed it "Madison Lake," incorrectly assuming it to be the source of the Madison River. In 1872 the correct drainage of the lake was discovered, and at a later date it was dubbed Shoshone Lake. (DeLacy received partial recognition when the stream which flows into Shoshone Lake from the north was named DeLacy Creek.)

The entire trip from DeLacy Creek trailhead to the South Entrance Road opposite Lewis Lake measures 13 mi., and can be made in a single day. This represents the shortest, most direct route, following the shorelines of Shoshone and Lewis lakes. It is obvious, then, that for greater enjoyment it would be wise to explore Shoshone Lake and camp at least 1 night along the way. Indeed, several days could be used to explore the wilderness of Shoshone Lake, which covers about 12 sq. mi. The Shoshone Geyser Basin at the far west end of the lake features an extensive number of hot springs and geysers, and it is a very rewarding area to canoe.

Shoshone Lake provides fishing opportunities for lake, brown, and brook trout. The lake, or mackinaw, was first planted in Lewis and Shoshone lakes in 1890. The park distribution of the lake trout, which may reach a weight of more than 30 lbs., is limited to Lewis, Shoshone and Heart lakes, and the Heart, Lewis, and Snake rivers. In the summer months, mackinaw remain in the deep cold waters of the lake, but they come into the shoal areas during October and November to spawn.

When you first enter the Lewis River from Shoshone Lake the current is moderate and will move you along at a nice rate. But shortly thereafter it practically disappears, and you will have to hand propel yourself the rest of the way to Lewis Lake. The Lewis River between Shoshone and Lewis lakes is actually a channel, since the elevations of the 2 lakes vary by only 12 ft. The junction of Lewis River and Lewis Lake marks the boundary beyond which motor-propelled boats are prohibited. As you enter Lewis Lake there is a good view to the east of Mt. Sheridan (10,308 ft.). Follow the shore around the north end of Lewis Lake to the South Entrance Road and watch for wildlife here, as there are several meadows along this stretch.

TRAILS FROM OLD FAITHFUL AREA

Old Faithful Visitor Center
to Observation Point   (0.8 mi.)

From the Visitor Center the trail passes around the east side of Old Faithful, then crosses the Firehole River at the 0.3 mi. mark. From the north side of the river a spur trail leads up to Observation Point, 0.5 mi. away. This trail is well marked and quite popular, as it leads up the forested ridge to a rock outcropping which provides a bird's-eye view of the famous geyser. There is an observation stand located here. Much has been written about Yellowstone's most famous attraction, but the best way to appreciate it is to see it in action. There are many geysers in the park that erupt to impressive size, but most people consider Old Faithful the star of Yellowstone's geyser show. Unfortunately, some people come away somewhat disillusioned; this may be the result of too much advance publicity. If you really want to observe Old Faithful at its best, come at sunrise. It is a magnificent sight.

Summit Lake Trail
(Biscuit Basin to Summit Lake)   (7.5 mi.)

Start from Biscuit Basin, located on the Madison-Old Faithful Road, 2 mi. from Old Faithful and 14 mi. from Madison. There is a parking lot provided here, and a footbridge across the Firehole River leads to the trailhead, located on the far side of Biscuit Basin. The Summit Lake Trail follows the Mystic Falls Trail for a short distance, then forks off to the left. The next 0.3 mi. takes you through a low-lying meadow and across the Little Firehole River. The trail then begins a long, steady climb, 7 mi. to Summit Lake. From this point on, the trip is not recommended. The trail climbs about 1,300 ft. through dry and uninteresting lodgepole forest to Summit Lake. There is no drinking water along the way, and the lake contains no fish, though it is worth a visit for those willing to endure the very strenuous hike.

Summit Lake is appropriately named, as it is located just to the east of the Continental Divide at 8,553 ft. For the most part, the trail follows an intermittent stream which serves as the outlet to Summit Lake, but by mid-July it is completely dry except for occasional stagnant pools. After you have climbed to about 8,200 ft. and are halfway to the lake, you will notice obsidian along the trail. Obsidian is a natural black volcanic glass, which was formed by a volcanic flow of rhyolite that cooled so quickly it did not crystallize. The glass substance contains very sharp edges which can cut you if not handled carefully. Indians made knives, arrowheads, and spears out of it.

Summit Lake is quite large, surrounded mostly by lodgepole forest, with a small meadow on the south end. From here it is 8.4 mi. to the western park boundary and the West Boundary Trail used for border patrol. (This hike runs through dry and uninteresting country across the Madison Plateau, and is not recommended.) For those who complete the strenuous trip to Summit Lake, it is worthwhile to continue about 1 mi. past the lake to a second, shallower lake on the south side of the trail that contains numerous hot springs. Just beyond this, on the north side of the trail, is another lake which is beautiful and quite deep. The water temperature varies from cool to warm in different areas.

Mystic Falls Trail
(Biscuit Basin to Mystic Falls)   (0.9 mi.)

The trail starts in Biscuit Basin, 2 mi. north from Old Faithful on the Grand Loop Road. There is a loop parking lot on the west side of the road here. A footbridge crosses the Firehole River, beyond which boardwalks traverse the area. One of the boardwalks leads past Sapphire Pool to the Mystic Falls trailhead located on the west side of the basin. The trail follows the Little Firehole River 0.9 mi. all the way to the falls. The wildflowers along the way—especially Indian paintbrush—are superb. Toward the end of the trail you will see several impressive cascades. Be sure to continue past these up the switchbacks to the overlook for the view of Mystic Falls, a 70 ft. drop.

Fairy Creek Trail
(Biscuit Basin to Fairy Creek)   (13 mi.)

The trailhead is located at Biscuit Basin, 2 mi. north from Old Faithful on the Grand Loop Road. There is a loop parking lot on the west side of the road here. A footbridge crosses the Firehole River, beyond which boardwalks traverse the Biscuit Basin area. One boardwalk leads by Sapphire Pool (a blue-green pool that at one time used to erupt to over 100 ft.) to the actual trailhead on the west side of the basin. From here, trails lead to Mystic Falls and Summit Lake, in addition to Fairy Creek.

Within the first 1.5 mi. the trail climbs through lodgepole pine and on up to 8,200 ft. at the 3 mi. mark, then descends about 350 ft. to the Little Firehole River, and at 5 mi. enters Little Firehole Meadows. This is an ideal grazing spot for wild animals, especially moose and elk. There are brown and rainbow trout in the Little Firehole River here, but this far upstream you may have trouble hooking one of appreciable size.

Three unnamed forks come together in the Little Firehole Meadows to form the headwaters of the Little Firehole River. The trail climbs gently out of the Little Firehole Meadows and continues through lodgepole pine to the headwaters of Fairy Creek, at the 8.5 mi. mark. At 9 mi. you will reach the edge of Madison Plateau, from which

Fairy Falls plunges only 1 mi. away to the east. Twin Buttes at 7,923 ft. and 7,865 ft. (S and N, respectively) are directly ahead. The trail descends from the plateau and passes below south Twin Butte. The Twin Buttes are actually hills of glacial drift that were cemented by siliceous sinter resulting from pre-glacial geyser and hot spring action. There are several active fumaroles on both hills. The earthquake of 1959 initiated apparent massive slumping which created several large steaming fissures as much as 15 ft. deep on both hills. Some of these fissures are now active fumaroles. There are several ponds located at the base of Twin Buttes.

Below south Twin Butte the trail passes by Imperial Geyser (see *Fairy Falls-Imperial Geyser Trail*). From here it is 3.1 mi. to the Firehole River bridge.

Fairy Falls-Imperial Geyser Trail   (3.1 mi.)

Fairy Falls and Imperial Geyser can be reached by starting either at the end of the Fountain Flat Drive at Goose Lake or at the Firehole River bridge. You can reach the bridge by driving 0.2 mi. along a short spur from the Grand Loop Road.

From the Firehole River bridge, the trail passes below the edge of the Madison Plateau and enters a spruce and fir forest, with many thermal features along the first mile. At 2.3 mi. you will come to the short spur trail that leads to the foot of Fairy Falls. Here the trees are quite large, and the rich forest undergrowth consists of various ferns and mosses and wildflowers. Fairy Falls at a height of 200 ft. is a graceful waterfall.

The trail reaches Imperial Geyser (via a short spur trail)

at 3.1 mi. Imperial Geyser, which rises out of a large crater about 150 ft. across and filled with boiling water, is in eruption about four-fifths of the time. After the beginning of each eruption water may shoot up to 40 ft., but the average height is 5 to 15 ft. The eruptions occur from 1 small area of the crater and last 5 to 10 min. Just north of Imperial Geyser are the Twin Buttes.

From Fairy Falls it is possible to continue north along the old Fairy Creek Trail and meet the Fountain Flat Drive at Goose Lake. This trail follows Fairy Creek through a dry meadow containing numerous hotspots. Bison are often spotted in this area. When you have traveled 2 mi. north, you will come to a spur trail leading westward to the Queens Laundry and Sentinel Meadow, 1.5 mi. away.

Fern Cascades Loop Trail   (3 mi.)

The east leg of the loop trail can be reached by following the Lone Star Geyser Trail from Old Faithful Ranger Station to the Fern Cascades Trail junction, or you can take the western loop, beginning from the Old Faithful government trailer court. From the Ranger Station you walk 0.7 mi. before a trail forks off to the right leading to Fern Cascades 1.5 mi. away. If you take the entire loop trail, the distance is about 3 mi.

Mallard Lake Trail
(Old Faithful to Mallard Lake)   (3.5 mi.)

The trailhead for this hike has recently changed. It is now located on the first Old Faithful Lodge cabin road coming in from the right as you drive into the lodge area. The trail actually begins 330 yds. down the cabin road. (If the trailhead is not marked, inquire at the Visitor Center.)

This trip takes you over rolling hills through a lodgepole pine forest to Mallard Lake. During the months of June, July, and early August it provides an excellent area for viewing wildflowers. At 0.2 mi. the Firehole River is crossed on a new footbridge constructed in 1972. At 0.4 mi. you will notice a small thermal area to the left of the trail which contains a mudpot, a large hot pool, and other, smaller features. Because of the thin crust here, you should be careful in approaching the area. The largest concentration of Douglas fir along the way is noted at the 1 mi. mark.

At the 2.2 mi. mark the trail enters a narrow canyon high on the left side, but gradually drops to meet the canyon floor. The scenery becomes spectacular through this gorge, especially when (at 2.6 mi.) you pass through a narrow defile with large boulders scattered on both sides. High up on the left is a cliff face showing twisted ancient lava flows, and from the right, on top of an exposed cliff, it is possible to view distant parts of the Upper Geyser Basin. Old Faithful can be seen erupting from here. (This observation point is 0.25 mi. from the trail and can be reached from 100 yds. further uptrail.)

Mallard Lake does not become visible until you are almost upon it. A steep timbered ridge slopes away from the southeast shore of the lake, providing a good spot from which to take photos. Cutthroat trout once thrived, but now the lake seems to be barren. There is usually a variety of birdlife on the lake's waters.

Old Fountain Pack Trail
(Lower Geyser Basin to West Entrance Road)   (13 mi.)

This trail begins from the Fountain Flat Drive (0.2 mi. from where the northern end joins the Grand Loop Road), climbs across the Madison Plateau, and comes out at the West Entrance Road approximately 4.5 mi. from the West Entrance. It follows a horse trail to West Yellowstone, and contains very little in the way of scenic attractions, so it is not recommended. The route climbs almost 1,000 ft. up on the Madison Plateau to its high point of 8,070 ft. at about the halfway mark. Most of the plateau is very dry, containing few streams and lakes, and very little undergrowth in the lodgepole pine forest. When the snow has melted, the streams all but disappear.

The Promontory and Yellowstone Lake

Thorofare Region

The Thorofare can appropriately be termed Yellowstone's premier wilderness region. The Snake and Upper Yellowstone rivers are among the chief streams; Heart and Yellowstone lakes are the major bodies of water; extensive meadows abound—particularly in the southeast corner; the craggy peaks of the Absarokas to the east are most impressive. The region is the summer home for a great many elk. Members of both the Jackson Hole and the Northern Yellowstone herds summer in the Snake River and Upper Yellowstone areas.

The number of backpackers who travel deep into Thorofare is small. Most of the travel is by horseback. The size of this area forces special considerations on backpackers planning extended visits. A week or more is required if you wish to travel deep into the southeast corner of the park, so plan accordingly when assessing miles-per-day, weight of pack (types of food, etc.), and comfortable gear (boots, etc.). In the southeast corner you will be over 30 mi. from the nearest road.

Most of the Thorofare is impassable in early summer due to high waters, so you should plan your trip for no earlier than July 15 for best results. The Indian Summer is a particularly good time to visit because the many meadows are tinted a beautiful gold, and the high peaks are often frosted

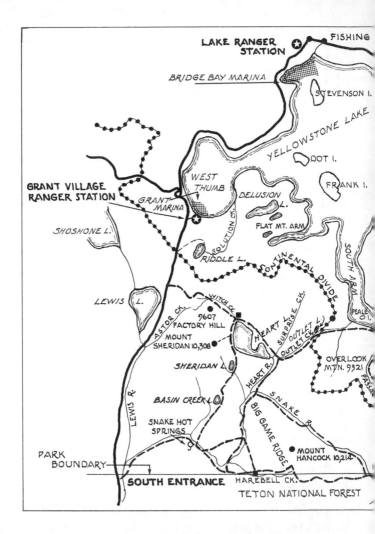

with white, and the elk are in rut. The region also encom-
passes Yellowstone Lake which offers a wilderness paradise
for canoeists venturing into the Southeast, South, and Flat
Mountain arms. (Note that the fishing season in the lake
opens several weeks earlier than that for many streams of
the Upper Yellowstone drainage. Current fishing regulations may be obtained from any ranger station or visitor
center.)

There are several possible routes for touring the Thorofare. You can make a number of wide loops of the region or
you can travel straight through, crossing over the park
boundary into the Teton Wilderness. One of the most beautiful trips in Yellowstone, and the best in Thorofare, begins
from the Eagle Creek trailhead (in Shoshone National Forest) on the Cody-East Entrance Road, 7 mi. from the East
Entrance, and goes up Eagle Creek, through the Eagle Creek
Meadows, and over Eagle Pass into Yellowstone Park. You
then descend the Howell Fork of Mountain Creek to Mountain Creek itself, and down Mountain Creek to the Upper
Yellowstone River. From here you enter the "true Thorofare," ascend Lynx Creek on the South Boundary Trail over
Two Ocean Plateau to Mariposa Lake, and proceed down to
the Snake River. The South Boundary Trail then takes you
over Big Game Ridge to Harebell Creek, up to Heart Lake,
and out at the South Entrance Road. This trip covers about
85 mi., requires perhaps 2 weeks, and offers some of the
grandest scenery to be found anywhere.

THOROFARE REGION TRAILS

❈ Thorofare Trail   (34 mi.)

Lake Butte trailhead (also called Ten-Mile Post), on the south side of the East Entrance Road, 10 mi. east of Fishing Bridge, is the starting point for Thorofare Trail. From the East Entrance Road, the trail descends steeply into a fine grove of spruce and fir. Cub Creek is crossed at 1.5 mi., and at 2 mi. the Clear Creek Trail junction is reached. From here, the Clear Creek Trail follows Clear Creek up to Sylvan Lake. The junction can be rather confusing as an old horse trail also joins it at this point, so make certain of the 3 forking trails by looking for orange trail markers (which the old horse trail does not have), and then take the right (SW) fork, which continues toward Thorofare. The trail crosses Clear Creek at 3 mi.; here a spur trail leads to a patrol cabin 0.5 mi. to the west. Unless you take this trail or walk through the trees down to the shore, you will not see Yellowstone Lake until you reach Park Point. Unfortunately, the Thorofare Trail along Yellowstone Lake's Southeast Arm provides only occasional views of the lake. It was apparently designed for horse travel down to Thorofare and not for scenic value.

As you approach the Park Point patrol cabin area from

the north, you come first to a meadow that is a popular spot for elk. The trail continues across this meadow, but the right fork leads over to the cabin area on the shore (about 0.5 mi.), with superb views of the lake. There is a designated campsite here. From Park Point you can witness a spectacular sunset over Yellowstone Lake. Frank Island lies directly to the west, with Dot Island just northwest of Frank, Promontory looming directly to the south, Flat Mountain to the southeast, the upper half of Mt. Sheridan also to the southeast, and portions of the Absaroka Range to the south. Immediately south of the cabin is a lagoon in which cutthroat trout are frequently trapped by a sand dam. Meadow Creek empties into the lake a few 100 yds. to the south of the cabin. The mouth of the creek here is actually a wide slough, and in June and early July you can see cutthroat trout spawning.

For the next 2 mi. beyond Park Point, the trail skirts along the lake's edge—though high above it—and the views themselves are worth the hike. Promontory rises directly across from you, and the entire shape of the Southeast Arm unfolds before you to the south. The huge meadow region at the southern tip of the arm (the mouth of the Upper Yellowstone River) is faintly visible.

Shortly before crossing Columbine Creek you will once again come to the lake's shore, at which point Mt. Doane (10,656 ft.) with its snowcap is partially visible to the west. (It is named in honor of Lt. Gustavus C. Doane, who was the commander of the military escort that accompanied the 1870 Washburn Expedition, and who wrote the first official report on Yellowstone. He also served with the Hayden Survey of 1871, and explored the Jackson Hole area in 1876.)

Columbine Creek is crossed at the 9 mi. mark. (Note that the water here is not very good for drinking.) The trail continues to below the Brimstone Basin through stands of lodgepole pine with almost no undergrowth.

At the 15 mi. mark Terrace Point is reached. If you walk over to the lake's edge you will be rewarded with some excellent views. It is in this vicinity that the geological evidence was found which proves that Yellowstone Lake was once 160 ft. higher than it is today. A mile beyond Terrace Point the trail swings into the open. The delta region of the mouth of the Upper Yellowstone River is laid out before you, with the Molly Islands clearly visible to the southwest and Colter Peak (10,683 ft.) dominating the skyline to the southeast. The view of the mouth of the Upper Yellowstone, surrounded by extensive meadows, with numerous birds soaring overhead, is particularly enjoyable.

Colter Peak is named for John Colter, the first white man to visit Yellowstone's wonders, in 1807. Colter probably entered what is now Yellowstone Park by following Thorofare Creek to the Upper Yellowstone River. From here, he may have crossed the Continental Divide at Two Ocean Pass south of the present park boundary, or ascended Lynx Creek, which would have taken him by Mariposa Lake on his way to the south fork of the Snake River. On September 7, 1870, Lt. Gustavus C. Doane and Nathaniel P. Langford sketched the first known authentic map of Yellowstone Lake.

At the 17 mi. mark the mouth of Beaverdam Creek is reached. This is a rather popular camping area, since it is the cutoff point beyond which motorboats are not allowed. The crossing of Beaverdam Creek (by ford) is another mile beyond the mouth of the stream. From here Mt. Schurz is partially visible to the east. At 11,139 ft. it is the second highest peak in the park. Colter Peak is again in view to the southeast. (Mt. Schurz was named for Carl Schurz, Secretary of the Interior under President Hayes. This was actually the peak christened Mt. Doane by Washburn and Langford in 1870, though maps place the honor on another peak east of the Southeast Arm.)

When walking in the high willow brush, or anywhere in the Thorofare area for that matter, be sure to make a certain amount of noise, as it is a fact that grizzlies often use this trail. Chances are you will see some tracks along the trail—particularly between the Beaverdam Creek area and Thorofare Ranger Station. Grizzly tracks may be distinguished from those of a black bear by the indentations of the claws on the front paws. A grizzly's claws may extend up to 6 in., but a black's claws are curved and do not extend beyond the front paws. The distance between the holes, or "dots," made by the claws and the front paws will key you to the bear's species.

After leaving the willow brush beyond Beaverdam Creek, the trail re-enters lodgepole pine. As you near the 20 mi. mark, a short loop trail leads down to Cabin Creek patrol cabin. (Just below the cabin to the west is a delightful, ice-cold stream.) Be sure to follow this trail on down to the Upper Yellowstone River (0.2 mi. away) as the wild beauty of this area is indeed special. Look for elk and moose in the meadows here. The trail leading down to the river is actually the Trail Creek Trail, which ends at Cabin Creek cabin, where it joins the Thorofare Trail.

About 1 mi. south of Cabin Creek the trail passes through dense spruce and fir. At the 23 mi. mark Trappers Creek is crossed; 0.5 mi. south of the creek you will enter

Turret Mountain Meadow. From here there is a fine view of the extremely rugged Turret Mountain (10,995 ft.) to the east, and the Two Ocean Plateau to the west. Turret Mountain consists of volcanic conglomerate. When a climb by the Sierra Club was attempted in 1926, an overhanging cliff of very brittle material only 100 ft. from the summit prevented the hikers from reaching the top. At 25 mi. you will come to the Mountain Creek Trail junction (Eagle Pass Trail), located among lodgepole pine. Eagle Pass is 10 mi. to the northeast. Another mile brings you to the crossing of Mountain Creek, where Turret Mountain is once again in view to the northeast. During early summer, grizzlies are often seen in this area feeding on the spawning Yellowstone cutthroat trout. Just beyond the creek is the other Mountain Creek trail junction (lower cutoff trail) which leads to Eagle Pass.

As the trail continues southward it begins to enter more meadows, and the scenery is truly spectacular—you are now entering the "real" Thorofare. In 2 places the Upper Yellowstone River winds right next to the trail to offer a view of one of America's wildest and most beautiful streams. The Two Ocean Plateau looms as a backdrop to the west. The second meeting of river and trail (farthest south) at the 29 mi. mark requires a stop. The views include the Upper Yellowstone winding through the meadow, the massive Two Ocean Plateau rising 10,115 ft. just across the river to the west, and the sharp cliffs of the northern Trident immediately above you to the east. Looking back across the river to the southwest you can easily distinguish where Lynx Creek and the South Boundary Trail are located.

The northern fork of Cliff Creek is crossed at the 30 mi. mark, and 0.5 mi. beyond the trail enters another meadow affording more fine views. As you leave the meadow from this point and re-enter the forest, a cold spring is located just to the west of the trail. Immediately before the trail junction at 31.5 mi. you will cross Escarpment Creek. The southern Trident (10,631 ft.) lies to the east. The streambed is not permanent but takes on a new course almost every summer following the big floods, of which evidence can easily be noted here. From the trail junction across the stream a trail leads 0.5 mi. to Thorofare Ranger Station, located beneath the southern Trident. A ranger is normally stationed here throughout the summer.

From the ranger station 2 trails lead to Bridger Lake, 2 mi. away, located just across the park boundary in the Teton Wilderness. (For travel in this particular area around Bridger Lake it is strongly suggested that you order a 15-min. topo map of Two Ocean Pass, Wyoming, 1959, which you can get from U.S.G.S., Distribution Section, in Denver, Colorado. A Wyoming fishing license is required for any fishing you may do south of the park boundary.) The westernmost trail is probably the most scenic route, leading to the west corner of Bridger Lake. The fording of Thorofare Creek is no easy matter, as it is quite wide and deep most of the summer. The name should be Thorofare *River*. From Thorofare Creek to Bridger Lake, you walk through an extensive meadow that provides fine views of the Two Ocean Plateau to the west and Hawk's Rest to the south. The trail then crosses the park boundary, leads through a stand of lodgepole, and comes out in a corner of the famous 7 mi. long Yellowstone Meadow.

Although the Bridger Lake general vicinity is not technically included in the park's boundaries, it certainly is a part of the park for several reasons. The Upper Yellowstone

River rises only a few miles south of Bridger Lake, then flows through Yellowstone Meadow into the park. About 7 air miles southwest of Bridger Lake is famous Two Ocean Pass, where the first cutthroat trout apparently crossed over and started the unique population in Yellowstone Lake. Also at Two Ocean Pass, Two Ocean Creek makes its separation right on the Continental Divide, forking into Pacific Creek to the west and Atlantic Creek to the east. The area is rich in historical associations. Fur trappers used to trap along the Upper Yellowstone in the early 1800's. John Colter passed through here in 1807, and in 1830 the legendary Jim Bridger camped for a time at the lake which is now named in his honor, and also discovered Two Ocean Pass. Other fur trappers who visited this area in the 1830's were Milton Sublette, Joe Meek, Thomas Fitzpatrick, and Jedediah Smith. Their rather "easy" survival in the Yellowstone wilderness lends support to the old fur trappers' slogan: "A fur trapper is tough, or he is dead." You may want to climb Hawk's Rest, which provides a spectacular view of Bridger Lake, the Upper Yellowstone River, and Yellowstone Meadow.

Clear Creek Trail (10 mi.)

You start at the east end of Sylvan Lake, which is located on the East Entrance Road, 17 mi. from Lake Junction. The Clear Creek Trail provides splendid backcountry scenery yet is rarely taken. The jumping-off spot at Sylvan Lake (8,414 ft.) is one of the more beautiful areas to be found along the road in the park, with Top-Notch Peak (10,238 ft.) to the east as a backdrop. The trail skirts the length of the lake on the southwest side. At 1.5 mi. it emerges into a meadow through which Clear Creek flows. Grizzly Peak at 9,948 ft. is in full view to the south. For the remainder of the hike, the trail continues to follow Clear Creek through dense woods, descending about 700 ft. to its junction with the Thorofare Trail at the 10 mi. point.

Mountain Creek Trail (Eagle Pass Trail)   (10 mi.)

The starting point is at Thorofare Trail Junction. This trail follows Mountain Creek (incorrectly shown as Monument Creek on some maps) for a short distance, then takes the Howell Fork up to near Eagle Pass (10 mi.). The climb up to the pass is almost 2,000 ft. Turret Mountain, Table Mountain, and Eagle Peak (all about 11,000 ft.) provide constant mountain scenery to the west, but also block out any possible views of Yellowstone Lake as you approach the pass. Eagle Pass (9,628 ft.) runs to the east of Eagle Peak, which at 11,358 ft. is the highest peak in Yellowstone. Some of the most beautiful views of the Absaroka Range are visible as you cross over Eagle Pass and enter Shoshone National Forest. The Forest Service Eagle Creek Trail then joins and continues 18 mi. to exit at the Cody Highway, 7 mi. east of the East Entrance. Although not currently maintained, an old outfitter trail follows Mountain Creek (the Eagle Pass Trail follows the Howell Fork) across the boundary and up to a 10,900 ft. pass (a distance of about 8 mi.), which provides access to the U.S.F.S. trail that descends Fishhawk Creek. The distance is 20 mi. from the pass out to the Cody Road, where the trail terminates 10 mi. east of the East Entrance. The scenery is spectacular along this route, but since the trail is not maintained from the Howell Fork up to the pass, you may expect downed timber and rockslides. This is wild mountain country, and an accident can be serious, so use good judgment in deciding on such an excursion.

☙ South Boundary Trail (39 mi.)

This trail begins at the South Entrance to the park. Most backpackers making extended trips into the Thorofare country from the South Entrance Road begin at the Heart Lake Trail; however, if the Snake River route is your objective, you can begin at the South Entrance. Most of the summer the Snake River is too deep to ford safely at the South Entrance; in this case, you can begin at the Snake River Bridge, located near Flagg Ranch (3 mi. south of the South Entrance gate). From here you follow the river along its eastern bank until you join the South Boundary Trail. (This adds about 3 mi.)

After crossing the river, the trail leads across a large meadow into a lodgepole forest. Around the 3.5 mi. mark you come to a bridge that extends through a dense growth of willows (you may see moose). There are occasional open areas along the way that contain many species of wildflowers. As you approach the 5 mi. mark and the Snake Hot Springs group, the scenery becomes very good. On first entering the meadow from the west you will come to a bridge that crosses a hot-flowing stream tinted a deep blue-green. The stream's source is located only a few yards away at a large hot spring. From the spring the blue-green stream flows beneath a large rock outcropping, then under the footbridge, and on into the Snake River. Across the river from these hotspots is a lake, apparently fed by an underground stream from the river. This lake is the only known water in the park's Snake River watershed that has not been invaded by exotic fish species. Due to the delicate balance between native species, *this lake is closed to fishing*.

At 6 mi. the Heart Lake Trail junction is reached. The cutoff trail appears at the 9 mi. mark at the head of a large meadow through which the Snake River flows. Another mile brings you to the junction of the Snake River Trail; at this point the Snake River courses to the northeast, leaving the South Boundary Trail. The South Boundary Trail crosses Harebell Creek a short distance beyond the junction. From the stream crossing, the trail climbs to Harebell patrol cabin, where a spur trail from the Snake River joins the South Boundary Trail. From the cabin a climb of 2,400 ft. begins to the top of Big Game Ridge, 7 mi. away at over 10,000 ft. For the first 3 mi. the trail continues along Harebell Creek. The timber in this stretch consists of large spruce and fir, and the undergrowth of ferns and mosses, berries, mushrooms, and many wildflowers, particularly harebell, Indian paintbrush, aster, and monkshood.

From the top of Big Game Ridge on a clear day the Absarokas to the east, the Tetons and Wind River ranges to the south, and the park's Gallatin Range to the northwest are all visible. Mt. Hancock, situated roughly in the middle of Big Game Ridge, lies directly to the north. (This peak, 10,214 ft., was climbed in 1871 by Captain J. W. Barlow, who named it after General W. S. Hancock, Commander of the Military Department.) It is a rare day when several elk are not spotted somewhere on Big Game Ridge. Note the change in species of trees. Much of the trail over the ridge skirts south of the park boundary into Teton National Forest, but there are adequate trail marker signs. Big Game Ridge is subject to quite severe weather conditions, particularly in September and October.

When you complete your descent from Big Game Ridge, the Snake River and Valley at the confluence of Fox Creek open before you. The Snake River Trail joins the South Boundary Trail at the river. Fox Creek patrol cabin is located on the South Boundary Trail east of the river. An unnamed stream flows behind the cabin; this is often mistaken for Fox Creek, which joins the Snake River right on the park boundary, near the South Boundary-Snake River trail junction. From Fox Creek cabin there is a U.S.F.S. trail leading southward to Fox Park patrol cabin. You may want to take time to walk down this, as it is only 0.5 mi. to Fox Park, a very large and beautiful meadow through which the Snake River meanders, and where Plateau Creek flows into the Snake. From Fox Creek cabin the trail crosses a meadow, then enters lodgepole. The Two Ocean Plateau Trail junction is reached at the 27 mi. mark (3 mi. east of Fox Creek cabin). From here, the trail climbs 500 ft. in 1 mi. to Mariposa Lake, at about 9,100 ft. The lake sits in a small depression, with meadows tinted purple by thousands of monkshood sloping away on the east, south and west sides. The northern shore is mostly wooded, and there are a few patches of timber surrounding the lake, which appears quite shallow. At such a high elevation (the Continental Divide is only about 1 mi. away to the east), it is surprising that it supports a small population of cutthroat trout.

The trail continues to climb to the Continental Divide, where a large meadow is entered for the start of the beautiful descent down Lynx Creek. From the divide there is a wonderful view of the Absaroka Range to the east. Shortly beyond the divide, the headwaters of Lynx Creek appear. The trail and creek then enter a spruce and fir forest, and

begin their descent of 1,500 ft. to the Yellowstone River.
There you are deep in the wilderness, over 30 mi. from the
road in any direction. As you follow Lynx Creek down to
the Yellowstone River, you will pass through dense spruce
and fir forest with thick underlying vegetation. The trail
crosses Lynx Creek many more times than is indicated on
the topo map. Occasional views of the 10,000 ft. ridge of
Two Ocean Plateau to the south appear along the way
down. When you reach the Upper Yellowstone River at
Yellowstone Meadow, you will be on the threshold of some
of Yellowstone's wildest and most beautiful backcountry
scenery. The trail parallels the Upper Yellowstone River for
a short distance, offering spectacular views of the Trident
and Turret mountains to the east. The sheer Two Ocean
Plateau directly west of the river is interrupted only by a
green slope halfway up the cliff. To the south, Hawk's Rest
can be seen east of the river. The 3 arms of the Trident are
in full view to the east. The ford is not too bad since it is
upstream from where Thorofare Creek empties into the
Yellowstone. The South Boundary Trail ends at Thorofare
Creek where it joins the Thorofare Trail. Bridger Lake is 1
mi. to the south from this junction.

Snake River Trail   (18 mi.)

The Snake River Trail starts 10 mi. east of South Entrance.
The Snake River Trail from the junction of Harebell Creek
to the junction of Fox Creek is not highly recommended
for hiking. Essentially a horse trail, it contains many need-
less ups and downs, and crosses the river back and forth
over a dozen times. While much of the scenery along the
river is indeed beautiful, the views are constantly limited by

forested, sloping ridges on both sides of the trail. More important, the South Boundary Trail over Big Game Ridge and the Trail Creek Trail from Heart Lake are certainly more desirable routes for traversing the Thorofare area. Highlights of the Snake River Trail include several narrow rock gorges through which the Snake gushes, and the vicinity surrounding the confluence of the Heart and Snake Rivers, where there are several hot springs, a sizable meadow, and an impressive view of Mt. Sheridan.

✗ Heart Lake Trail   (17.4 mi.)

The trailhead is just north of Lewis Lake on the east side of the South Entrance Road, 7.4 mi. south of West Thumb. For the first 5 mi. the trail traverses gently rolling terrain through lodgepole pine. You then reach an overlook from which Witch Creek, the Heart Lake Geyser Basin and Heart Lake can be seen. Factory Hill (9,607 ft.) dominates the view to the south. (The mountain was named for its apparent resemblance, noted as early as 1829, on a frosty morning, to an early American factory town.) Factory Hill is the northern terminus to the Red Mountain Range, which occupies much of the land between Lewis and Heart lakes, with Mt. Sheridan (10,308 ft.) dominating. The Red Mountain Range derives its name from the prevailing color of the volcanic rocks; when exposed to sun, the porphyry becomes a dark red. Most of the range is completely timbered to the summit. In 1926 the Sierra Club held its Yellowstone outing in this area, and several climbs were made of peaks here and in the Absarokas along the eastern boundary. The trail descends to Witch Creek (named for the many thermal features along its course) and through a large meadow. A number of hot springs spill into the stream, raising the creek's temperature to 80°F. As a result, there are no trout except close to where it enters the lake.

Heart Lake patrol cabin is on the northwestern shore of the lake near the trail. There is usually a fire control aide here during the summer months who should be able to give you up to date information on trail conditions and the fishing. Heart Lake contains cutthroat and lake trout. The lake trout (or mackinaw) grow quite big here, but are difficult to catch. (The largest one ever caught in Yellowstone weighed 43 lbs., and was caught several years ago at Heart Lake.) The big fish live in very deep water during the summer months, but come into the shallow areas in October and November to spawn.

There are several fine campsites along the western and northern shores of the lake. Along the western shore (at the 8 mi. mark) is Rustic Geyser, which erupts up to 30 ft. every 30 to 90 min. In 1872, Dr. A. C. Peale of the Hayden Expedition found Rustic Geyser "bordered by logs which are coated with a crystalline, semi-translucent deposit of geyserite. These logs were evidently placed around the geyser by either Indians or Whitemen a number of years ago, as the coating is thick and the logs firmly attached to the surrounding deposit." Sunrise over Heart Lake begins just as the moon disappears behind Mt. Sheridan. The sight is unforgettable.

The junction of the Mt. Sheridan Trail is met just south of Rustic Geyser at 8.2 mi. The hike up the mountain is about 3 mi. The Tetons are to the south, the Pitchstone Plateau to the west and Heart Lake, Lewis Lake, Shoshone Lake and Yellowstone Lake can be seen. Mt. Sheridan was named by Captain Barlow of the 1871 expedition after

General Philip H. Sheridan, a distinguished soldier who often visited the park and worked for its interest. It was near Mt. Sheridan that Truman Everts, a member of the Washburn Party, was lost for 37 days in September, 1870.

As you continue along the western shore of Heart Lake below the east face of Mt. Sheridan, you will notice some distinctive avalanche chutes where tons of snow have roared down on the lake in past winters. During the winter of 1968, an avalanche of tremendous proportions swept away hundreds of tall trees here, depositing many in the lake.

Continuing beyond Heart Lake the trail passes Sheridan Lake in open country at the 11 mi. mark. Populations of mostly small cutthroat thrive here. Much of the trail passes through open country for the next 5 mi. Basin Creek is crossed at 12 mi. At 12.5 mi., the Basin Creek Cutoff Trail leading to the Snake River Trail (2 mi. away) is joined. Basin Creek Lake appears at 13 mi.—the fishing for cutthroat here is generally better than in Sheridan Lake. At Basin Creek Lake the trail re-enters timber for a short distance, then emerges into a sizable meadow through which Red Creek runs. The Snake River, with its wide gravel streambed, is reached at 17 mi., where a ford is required. You join the South Boundary Trail at 17.4 mi.

Trail Creek Trail   (22.2 mi.)

You can reach Heart Lake patrol cabin via the Heart Lake Trail from the South Entrance Road. The trail starts here. The Trail Creek Trail provides 22.2 mi. of truly gentle wilderness. It is very level for most of the way, with flowering meadows (ideal habitat for moose and elk), deltas, and sloughs.

From Heart Lake cabin the trail skirts the sandy beach along the north shore of the lake, enters a lodgepole forest, then emerges into the first of many fine meadows. Beaver Creek is crossed in this meadow at the 1.7 mi. mark.

At 4.5 mi. the Heart River Cutoff Trail provides access to the Snake River Trail 3 mi. south. Just beyond the trail junction is the confluence of Surprise and Outlet creeks, which unite to form a fork of the Heart River (the other fork is the outlet for Heart Lake). At the 6 mi. mark you will cross Outlet Creek at the foot of a long, narrow meadow, paralleled on both sides by high forested ridges. In a forested bowl at the head of the meadow lies Outlet Lake, the source for Outlet Creek. Prior to the Ice Age, this very meadow may well have been the outlet for Yellowstone Lake, emptying it into the Pacific Ocean. Eventually, the channel from Yellowstone Lake to Heart River dammed at the Continental Divide. Yellowstone Lake now drains into the Atlantic. From Outlet Lake you leave a body of water which eventually flows into the Pacific, and climb only 200 ft. in 0.5 mi. over the Continental Divide to Grouse Creek, which eventually flows into the Atlantic. This is one of the easiest divide crossings among the park's trails. Grouse Creek courses through another meadow toward the South Arm of Yellowstone Lake. To the north is Channel Mountain and to the south Overlook Mountain—both of which comprise portions of Chicken Ridge. At the 10 mi. mark the trail crosses Grouse Creek and bends away from the meadow and stream.

During early summer cutthroat trout spawn in the streams of this area; the activity attracts a variety of wildlife, including the grizzly bear. The southern shore of the South Arm sees its share of grizzlies all summer, and if you look along the sandy beaches here, chances are you will spot grizzly tracks. Across the bottom of the arm to the east lies Peale Island (see *Canoeing on Yellowstone Lake*).

Just short of 13 mi., the cutoff trail to the Two Ocean Plateau Trail is joined at the southernmost slough of the South Arm. This remote slough is actually a miniature arm of Yellowstone Lake itself, which contains moose, elk, and a variety of birdlife. Chipmunk Creek, another active trout-spawning stream, is crossed in a further meadow (14.3 mi.). At 15.2 mi., you will have reached the junction of the Two Ocean Plateau in a marshy meadow; here there is a shallow lake which usually sports a number of duck and occasionally trumpeter swan.

Trail Creek patrol cabin and the Southeast Arm appear at 17 mi. From here the trail skirts the shore of the lake for about 1 mi., then enters a large meadow at the mouth of Trail Creek. About 1 mi. upstream from where the trail crosses the creek is Trail Lake (seldom visited), nestled in dense timber. It contains populations of small cutthroat. The Upper Yellowstone River ford is reached at the 21.7 mi. mark; there are dropoffs in this area, so be careful to seek out a wide, shallow crossing. The best place to cross is upstream on the southernmost ford (on the cutoff trail to the Thorofare Trail, rather than directly to Cabin Creek cabin); here the stream is broader but less swift. Cabin Creek cabin and the Thorofare Trail are reached at the 22.2 mi. mark.

Two Ocean Plateau Trail (Passage Creek Trail)   (12 mi.)

Start at Trail Creek Trail, 1.8 mi. west of the patrol cabin. The Two Ocean Plateau Trail is seldom traveled. It dis-

appears from sight in several places where large open areas
are crossed, but orange trail markers show the way.

As the trail nears the confluence of Chipmunk and Passage creeks, you will emerge into a large burned-over area
known as the Chipmunk Burn. The fire occurred in 1941
and destroyed 11,000 acres of spruce, fir and lodgepole
forest. The heavily forested Two Ocean Plateau, along with
the Mirror Plateau, has been designated by the Park Service
as a backcountry area where *natural* forest fires will be
allowed to burn without man's interference, though under
close observation. This experimental program will hopefully
provide more information on the relationship between forest fires and forest reproduction and succession. The new
forest growth can be seen, as the entire burned-over area is
sprinkled with young timber. After crossing the Chipmunk
Burn, the trail enters a spruce and fir forest and begins a
steady climb up to the Continental Divide, reached around
the 9 mi. mark. After a steep climb up to the divide at over
9,200 ft., the trail actually follows the Continental Divide
for about 1 mi. Once on top, subalpine conditions prevail.
(Keep a close watch for the trail marker poles at this point.)
You may happen upon a large herd of elk in this area.

At the 11.6 mi. you will cross Plateau Creek. Approximately 1.2 mi. upstream from here is Plateau Falls (75 ft.)
which is rarely visited. The junction of the South Boundary
Trail is reached after 12 mi. Mariposa Lake is now only 1
mi. away to the east (see *South Boundary Trail*).

Riddle Lake Trail   (2.5 mi.)

Start at the South Entrance Road, 4.3 mi. south of Grant.
Riddle Lake is used by fishermen, as it is only 2 mi. to the

shore. The lake, which is the source for Solution Creek, is bordered to the west and south by large meadows, and holds good populations of cutthroat. (It is not a bad idea to pack in a rubber raft if you have one, so that you may reach the deeper areas, but be sure to obtain regulations.) During the years before the park's exploration (the 1870's) it was believed that there was a lake in this area which contained major drainages to both oceans. Once the actual location of the Continental Divide was determined, the "riddle" was solved, and the stream draining the lake was the "solution." Indeed, the Continental Divide is only 1 mi. away to the south and east, and is crossed just beyond the trailhead at the 0.2 mi. point.

CANOEING ON YELLOWSTONE LAKE

Perhaps one of the best ways to see and enjoy Yellowstone's wilderness with minimal effort is to explore the far reaches of Yellowstone Lake. There is probably no more beautiful sight in all Yellowstone than the lake at sunset as viewed from the west shore. F. V. Hayden wrote of Yellowstone Lake in 1871: ". . . a vast sheet of quiet water, of a most delicate ultramarine hue, one of the most beautiful scenes I have ever beheld. . . . The great object of all our labors had been reached, and we were amply paid for all our toils. Such a vision is worth a lifetime, and only one of such marvelous beauty will ever greet human eyes." The Southeast, South and Flat Mountain arms represent some of Yellowstone's finest wilderness scenery.

Before taking craft on the waters of Yellowstone Lake (or any other park waters), it is mandatory that you stop by Lake Ranger Station or Grant Village Ranger Station to register it. You will receive a boat permit (no charge) and also some very important safety regulations which you should be aware of for your own protection (see *Briefed Boating Regulations*). Small craft should stay within 0.25 mi. of shore at all times. Yellowstone Lake is famous for its sudden storms and wind.

Early park explorers compared Yellowstone Lake to the shape of a man's left hand, although there are only 3 "fingers," or arms, to the lake. West Thumb derives its name from this early description. It is in these 3 arms of the lake that canoeists can best explore Yellowstone's wilderness scenery. There are several designated campsites along the shores. Motorboats are restricted here to 5 m.p.h. and are not allowed to operate at the arms' tips. Many people believe they should be discontinued altogether. The reasons are clear. The South and Southeast arms represent very wild portions of Yellowstone's wilderness. At the southern tips you are 12 to 16 mi. from the nearest road. Hopefully in the near future motorboats will be prohibited from all of Yellowstone Lake so that those who hike or canoe in will find the natural setting undisturbed.

From Yellowstone Lake the skyline will vary constantly with such backdrops as the mighty snow-capped Absarokas, Promontory, Flat Mountain, Mt. Sheridan, Chicken Ridge, and Two Ocean Plateau. A canoe trip up Flat Mountain arm is recommended, since the marshy meadow at the extreme tip is usually teeming with birdlife. Among the waterfowl you may expect to observe on Yellowstone Lake are the trumpeter swan, great blue heron, pelican, caspian tern, Canadian geese, cormorant, many species of duck, gull and other birds. Flat Mountain rises some 1,500 ft. from the arm's south shore. For the more hardy, a side trip to the top of Flat Mountain will provide breathtaking views toward the east of Yellowstone Lake, Promontory, and Absarokas.

The South Arm also provides excellent sightseeing and exploring. The most beautiful scenery lies near the upper southern tip. There are several sloughs in this region that invite further exploration. Peale Island is particularly beautiful. (Camping is not allowed on the island, though there is a cabin which is used for winter patrols and other administrative purposes.) The fishing, as in all the arms, is good for Yellowstone cutthroat trout. The mouth of Grouse Creek is an attractive area to explore, with a sizable meadow that often contains big game.

The Southeast Arm of Yellowstone is the largest, and perhaps the most beautiful—with the Absaroka Range in the background. Terrace Point, located on the east shore about two-thirds of the way up the southern tip of the arm, contains geological evidence of the former lake which once covered 310 sq. ml. (twice its present area), extending across much of the Hayden Valley clear to the base of Mt. Washburn, and was approximately 160 ft. higher than it is at present. These conditions existed at the height of the Ice Age melt-off. Located on Terrace Point is a series of old lake shoreline beaches that extend up the hillside; the highest shoreline mark is 160 ft. above the present beach. The shoreline contains several old beaches, indicating that the lake did not drain continuously, but in stages during which the water level remained stationary. It took 15,000 years for the lake to lower 160 ft.

The most beautiful section of the Southeast Arm is undoubtedly the southern tip, where the Upper Yellowstone River enters the lake. In this delta region, extensive meadows abound in wildlife. The area surrounding the mouth of Beaverdam Creek contains a great deal of willow brush, which moose favor. Of particular interest are the Molly Islands, located in the southwest end of the arm. The 2 islands, known as Sandy and Rocky, are little more than scraps of sand and rock. The combined areas equal only about 1 acre—certainly not much of a nesting space. Nevertheless, here is the only breeding colony of white pelicans in Wyoming, and the only one in a national park. The birds start arriving in April and May with snow and ice still present, and then begin to reproduce despite the ordeals of a cold, blustery spring. The hazards the young chicks must face are numerous; of every 5 eggs laid, only 1 will hatch a pelican that will reach maturity. The pelicans fly for the first time in August, and begin their fall migration in September. Studies involving banded birds show that pelicans from the Molly Islands fly across southwestern America to spend the winter in Mexico along the Pacific Coast. Pelicans consume an estimated 400,000 cutthroat trout every year from Yellowstone Lake. Boats are not allowed to approach the islands—regulations specify that boaters stay at least 0.25 mi. away—since the pelicans depend upon the remote conditions here for their successful breeding.

For those planning extensive trips into all the arms of Yellowstone Lake, it is advisable to allot from 10 to 12 days to 2 weeks as adequate time. Obtain current information on the lake at the Lake or Grant Village ranger stations before departing—it is always a good idea to write in advance, stating your plans. Here is some general information for your canoe trip. On Flat Mountain Arm, prevailing winds usually funnel up the arm each afternoon and create choppy conditions. Keep in mind when planning a trip into the upper arms (S and SE) that the journey to the mouths is a lengthy one. There are usually smooth water conditions for easy paddling before 11:00 A.M. and between 5:00 and 7:00 P.M.; the lake's waters are almost always too choppy during midday. Rather than paddle up the east shore of the South Arm (which often receives strong afternoon winds) around to the Southeast Arm, plan to beach at the *mouth* of Chipmunk Creek and portage across the meadow down to the trail which leads over to it. (Boating upstream is discouraged to protect an abundance of nesting waterfowl, as well as numerous beaver.)

Central Plateau Region

This region includes most of Hayden Valley, which is home to many elk that come here in the summer. Moose are commonly sighted, particularly close to the Canyon-Lake Road. Herds of bison usually spend the early part of the summer here, and individual bulls are a common sight throughout the valley. These tough beasts also spend the winter here, near a number of hot springs in the area. Furthermore, Hayden Valley is prime grizzly bear country. For this reason you should remain very alert while hiking, being careful not to surprise a bear along the trail. The grizzly ranks as one of the most magnificent animals in the world, and it is indeed unfortunate that his domain has now been reduced to Yellowstone and Glacier national parks and a few surrounding areas. Estimates of the grizzly population in Yellowstone range from 175 to 250. This amounts to only 1 bear per 14 sq. mi. throughout the park, but before you rule out the possibility of encountering one, you should realize that the grizzly often gathers in higher numbers in suitable habitats—such as Hayden Valley and Fawn Pass; also, grizzlies often range about, covering an extensive area in a short time. Park officials occasionally restrict the use of some trails when grizzlies appear to be unusually active. You will be informed of any such restrictions when you request a backcountry use permit.

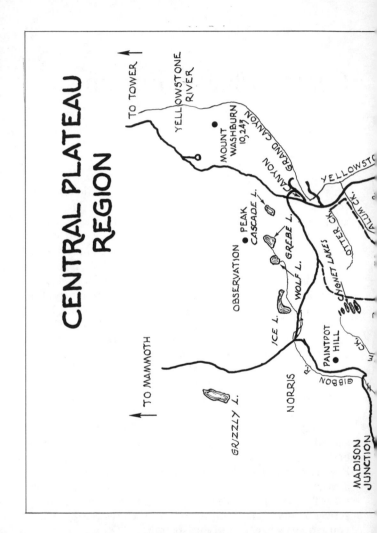

CENTRAL PLATEAU REGION

TO MAMMOTH

TO TOWER

YELLOWSTONE RIVER

MOUNT WASHBURN 10,243

GRAND CANYON

CANYON

YELLOWSTO

YELLOWSTONE

CASCADE L.

PEAK OBSERVATION

GREBE L.

WOLF L.

ICE L.

CYGNET LAKES

OTTER CR.

TUWACK

GRIZZLY L.

NORRIS

PAINTPOT HILL

GIBBON

GY

MADISON JUNCTION

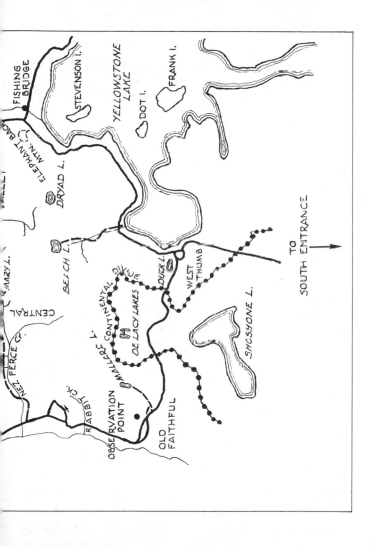

The Hayden Valley is also rich in history. It was through this region in 1877 that General Howard of the U.S. Army pursued the Nez Perce Indians, led by Chief Joseph. Although Chief Joseph was not a war-provoking chief, several renegade braves broke away from his tribe and bolted through the Hayden Valley, terrorizing a group of tourists visiting the park. George Cowan, the leader of the touring party from Radarsburg, Montana, was shot near Mary Mountain on Nez Perce Creek. His wife rushed to his aid but was dragged away by Indians, and another shot at close range struck Cowan in the forehead. He was left to die. The Indians finally released Mrs. Cowan and the rest of the party near Mud Volcano, from where they made it safely to Bozeman. Cowan began a slow crawl back to the party's Lower Geyser Basin camp 9 mi. away. A passing Indian spotted his movement and shot him in the side. Cowan managed to play dead until darkness and then, amazingly, continued back to camp. On August 28, four days later, he was found at the camp by 2 of General Howard's scouts, and his slow but dogged recovery began.

For most hikers traveling through the Central Plateau region the goal is Mary Lake, which lies roughly in the center of the wilderness region.

CENTRAL PLATEAU REGION TRAILS

Otter Creek to Mary Lake . . . . 12 mi.

Plateau Trail (Mary Lake to Norris-Canyon Road) . . 8 mi.

Mary Mountain Trail . . . . 11 mi.

Beach Lake Trail . . . . 5.5 mi.

Elephant Back Mountain Loop Trail . . . . 3.5 mi.

Artists Paintpots Trail . . . . 0.5 mi.

Otter Creek to Mary Lake   (12 mi.)

The old Otter Creek campground road, about 3 mi. south from Canyon Junction off the Canyon-Lake Road is the official starting point for this hike, but many choose to begin their trip out in the Hayden Valley where Alum Creek passes under the road, joining the Yellowstone River. This cuts off about 2 mi. and starts you out in the open valley right away. If you choose to do this, simply begin at or near Alum Creek and stay along the edge of the forest with the creek below you to the south. In less than 2 mi. you will join the Mary Mountain Trail. The trail never crosses Alum Creek, always staying on the north side of it until it approaches Highland Hot Springs. There you cross a small fork of the creek (this is about 10 mi. from Otter Creek). Immediately after entering the valley, you will follow Alum Creek through a narrow opening of trees. There are several hot springs along Alum Creek as it winds through the valley. A geyserite cone about 6 ft high near the junction of Violet Creek spouts a small but steady flow of water.

Bison, or buffalo, winter quite frequently in this area. Bison can be extremely dangerous if approached too closely—especially individual bulls—so you should be careful to keep your distance.

According to Jim Bridger, the Yellowstone contained a stream (Alum Creek) which when forded by elk caused their hooves to shrink to the size of those of an antelope. The shrinking properties of Alum Creek have yet to be proven, but one drink from this stream and you'll understand where Jim obtained his information—it's a taste you won't ever forget.

As you cross Violet Creek and begin to move away from Alum Creek, you will be approaching a forest to the west that provides excellent wildlife, including the grizzly bear. Most animals prefer this "edge effect" where forest and open land meet. As you enter the forest once again and leave the large grassland-sageland of Hayden Valley behind, Mary Lake is only about 3 mi. away to the west. Some 1.5 mi. from the lake you will cross a fork of Alum Creek which winds through a large open meadow to Highland Hot Springs. You may spot bison in the vicinity of these springs. Notice the number of big game tracks leading to and from Mary Lake. The trail continues around the north end of the Lake to a campsite on the west end near the patrol cabin. The National Park Service patrol cabin, of course, is for official use only and is locked at all times. There is a tree immediately behind the patrol cabin which contains some very large and obvious claw marks—probably made by a grizzly.

Mary Lake has no permanent inlet or outlet, and there are no fish populations here. There is usually some form of birdlife, with duck the most common; trumpeter swan are occasionally spotted here.

Plateau Trail (Mary Lake to Norris-Canyon Road)   (8 mi.)

Start from the south side of the Norris-Canyon Road, 5 mi. west of Canyon Junction, or from Mary Lake. This particular trail is the shortest route in to Mary Lake, but is not overly popular since it does not go through any portion of Hayden Valley. It is a good second leg to a trip through Hayden Valley, however, as the trailhead on the Norris-Canyon Road is not too far from Canyon Junction. The trail crosses the higher portions of the Central Plateau at 8,400 ft. and, with 1 exception, winds through a dense lodgepole pine forest. The exception is Cygnet Lakes and meadows at the halfway mark—4 mi. from Mary Lake. Here a large meadow contains a series of 5 lakes named after the young of trumpeter swan. The trumpeter once seemed hopelessly headed for extinction. In 1930, only 21 trumpeters were counted in the park. However, due to protection of their habitat both in and out of the park, the birds have made a strong comeback. Chances are good that you will see other rare birds in this vicinity, including the elegant sandhill crane. Beyond the lakes and meadow the trail continues through heavy lodgepole, part of which is an old forest fire burn. The trail meets the Norris-Canyon Road about 5 mi. from Canyon Junction.

✗ Mary Mountain Trail   (11 mi.)

This trail begins on the east side of the Madison-Old Faithful Road, 6 mi. south of Madison. It follows Nez Perce Creek through forest and meadow most of the way to Mary Lake. (This is the same route which General Howard used in 1877 to pursue the Nez Perce Indians.) At the 4.5 mi. mark it crosses a stream known as Cowan Creek in a fine meadow through which the Nez Perce runs. Cowan is named for George Cowan, as it was near here that he was first shot down.

The meadows in this area provide excellent habitat for big game, and bison are often spotted. Nez Perce Creek is full of brown and rainbow trout. (Mary Lake itself does not contain any fish.)

Beach Lake Trail   (5.5 mi.)

The trailhead is on the north side of the Lake Junction-West Thumb Road, 5.3 mi. from Grant. This trail is very rarely traveled. Except for some beautiful flower-laden meadows along the way, the scenery is confined to the familiar lodgepole forest. Arnica Creek, named for the yellow wildflower, is followed most of the way. It contains a few pan-sized cutthroat. Beach Lake is lined with meadows along the southern shore, and there are usually many birds on the lake and in the general vicinity. You may spot a pair of trumpeter swan spending the summer here.

Elephant Back Mountain Loop Trail   (3.5 mi.)

The trail begins behind the Lake Lodge cabins. Due to construction in this area, you should check with Lake Ranger Station or Fishing Bridge Visitor Center for current location of the trailhead. The primary attraction of this hike is the magnificent view of Yellowstone Lake from atop the ridge. The climb is about 750 ft. This trip is frequently included among the naturalist-conducted hikes offered by the Park Service. (Information may be obtained at Fishing Bridge Visitor Center.)

⚹ Artists Paintpots Trail   (0.5 mi.)

The trailhead is on the east side of the Norris-Madison Road, 4.2 mi. from Norris. I recommend this walk. It takes you to an out-of-the-way thermal area. It leads around the edge of a meadow and into a lodgepole pine forest. The many pots and pools vary in size and color. The first pools are a cloudy blue, due to colloidal silica; the very fine particles suspended in the pools give the water a somewhat milky hue. Nearby are red-brown pools and a clear green one. As you proceed up the hill, you will notice the varied sounds—fumaroles roaring, pools splashing, and mudpots bubbling. Boardwalks are provided here for your safety, so do not take chances by approaching too closely, as thin crust could give way.

Electric Peak

Gallatin Region

The Gallatin Region provides excellent opportunities for high mountain hiking, as the Gallatin Range, with its 19 peaks stretching from south to north, is the featured attraction. The range is actually only about 20 mi. in length; Electric Peak (nearly 11,000 ft.) marks the northernmost point (and the highest) and Mt. Holmes (10,336 ft.), the southernmost. The mountains are part of an uplifted block of stratified shales, limestones, and sandstones dipping slightly northward. The forces of erosion slowly carved this raised block to form the present peaks and cirques. Since the rock layers dip northward, the younger and higher beds are found in Electric Peak, and the older layers are exposed on Mt. Holmes.

The major streams of this region include the Gallatin and Gardner rivers, located to the west and east of the Gallatin Range, respectively, and the Madison River, located in the southwest corner of the region. The Gardner River and Gardners Hole (not to be confused with the town of Gardiner) were named for Johnson Gardner, a fur trapper for the American Fur Company in 1832.

In the extreme northwest corner of the park is an area containing rugged peaks, dominated by Bighorn Peak, a petrified forest, and a number of beautiful high mountain lakes.

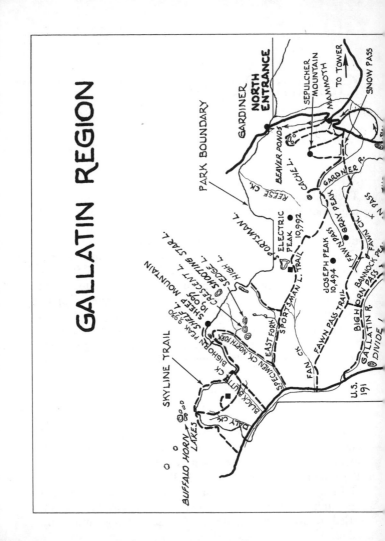

GALLATIN REGION

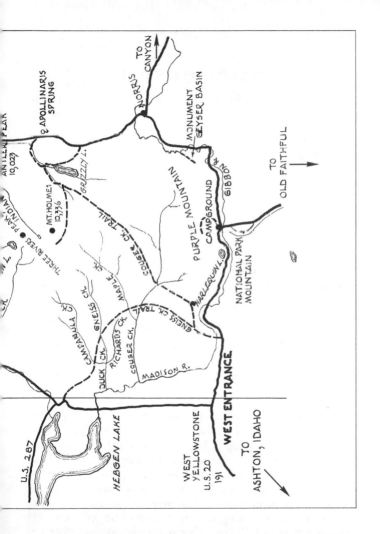

GALLATIN REGION TRAILS

Bighorn Peak Trail (Skyline Trail)　　　　　(15 mi.)

The starting point is U.S. 191 at Black Butte Creek cross-ing, 2.4 mi. inside the north boundary. Black Butte Creek lies to the northwest of the very conspicuous Black Butte. The hike up to the top of Bighorn Peak must rank as one of the most strenuous in the park, as you gain over 3,000 ft. in only 6 mi.—the last 4.5 mi. climbing 2,330 ft. Once the Skyline Trail is joined, though, your efforts will be re-warded with some very rugged mountain scenery. At about the 3 mi. mark during the steep climb you will enter the Gallatin Petrified Forest. This is interesting, but does not compare with the standing petrified forest on Specimen Ridge (see *Specimen Ridge Trail*). As you near the summit of Bighorn Peak, the trail becomes difficult to follow, and you will need to look closely for orange trail markers or rockpiles. The summit seems much higher than 9,930 ft. The view is magnificent in all directions from this bare and exposed place, particularly of the snowcapped peaks of the Madison Range to the northwest.

The Skyline Trail is joined near the summit. To the east, the trail follows the ridge right on the park boundary for a distance of 8 mi. To the west, it continues to the Shelf Lake, 3 mi. away. As you descend several 100 ft. from the summit, the trail follows a series of switchbacks with some very steep dropoffs nearby. *It is strongly suggested that you remain on the trail in this very rugged and potentially dangerous area.* One hiker fell to his death here in 1969. As you follow the ridge along the park boundary to Shelf Lake, note the scraggly growths of whitebark pine which grow at these high elevations; there are also fine views of the Gallatin Range along the way. About halfway from Bighorn Peak to Shelf Lake, Crescent Lake can be spotted in the distance to the southeast, sitting at the foot of a cirque. To the northeast is prominent Sheep Mountain (10,095 ft.), with its conspicuous relaying equipment perched on top. Watch for the bighorn sheep while on the Skyline Trail.

At the 8.7 mi. mark the trail drops down from the ridge to Shelf Lake, located at nearly 9,200 ft. If you continue on the ridge above Shelf Lake, the trail will take you to the summit of Sheep Mountain. From the lake you may want to take the time to climb the grassy ridge to the north, which has a fine view of Ramshorn Peak to the northwest (10,289 ft.) and also a very beautiful bird's-eye view of

Shelf Lake itself. From the top of this ridge the rather poorly marked Skyline Trail continues to the summit of Sheep Mountain.

From Shelf Lake the trail descends from 1,400 ft. in 2 mi. to the North Fork Specimen Creek at the 11 mi. mark. There you must decide whether you want to make an extensive loop hike of the Gallatin region. If you continue up to Crescent Lake, you will find the trail barely marked beyond it. In fact, for all practical purposes it disappears. You will make better time if you descend the North Fork Specimen Creek Trail around Meldrum Mountain and then follow the Sportsman Lake trail along the east fork of Specimen Creek. As it is only 1.5 mi. up to Crescent Lake you may want to drop your pack and make a side trip—a climb of 850 ft. There is a campsite and a small latrine here at the lake's outlet. Alpine lakes such as Shelf and Crescent are fragile environments, and proper camping techniques become very important. Crescent Lake was stocked with trout years ago, but it is now barren. From Crescent Lake, the trail does *not* continue past Sedge and Crag lakes as depicted on the U.S.G.S. topo map; instead, it makes a wide loop around the ridges to the northeast of Sedge Lake and then disappears.

Sedge Lake can be reached by bending away from the present trail past Crescent Lake and following the old trail eastward. Crag Lake is only 0.5 mi. to the southeast of Sedge Lake. Both lakes provide beautiful scenery but poor fishing.

Sportsman Lake Trail   (25 mi.)

From the west, the trail begins from Specimen Creek on U.S. 191, 5 mi. inside the north boundary. From the east, it begins at Mammoth-Norris Road, 2.5 mi. south of Mammoth. Specimen Creek is a forest trail. The North Fork Specimen Creek Trail, which provides access up to Crescent and Shelf lakes, is passed at the 2 mi. mark. The High Lake Trail is crossed at 6.5 mi.; from this point to Sportsman Lake, the trail is very muddy during wet weather, and can get quite slippery on the steep rises. Sportsman Lake appears at the 11 mi. mark. A large meadow runs all around the south end of the lake, and to the northwest a steep ridge rises some 1,200 ft. A few miles away to the east is Electric Peak. A large boulder on the eastern shore, known as Yahoo Rock, provides a fine overview of the lake.

In the meadow south of the lake there is a trail junction. To the north is the Mol Heron Creek Trail, which crosses the park boundary and extends into the Gallatin National Forest. This trail crosses the boundary 2 mi. to the north and reaches a remote dirt road at about 6 mi. The Sportsman Lake Trail continues to the south up and over the saddle to the southwest of Electric Peak. It is a long, hard climb (2,100 ft.) to the top of this saddle. About three-fourths of the way up is a splendid view of Sportsman Lake. Notice the weatherbeaten, scraggly growths of lodgepole and whitebark pine as you near the timberline. Above the timberline you may be able to see bighorn sheep. From the top of the saddle, at over 9,800 ft., continue to follow the ridge to the northeast if you wish to climb to the summit of Electric Peak. However, the view will not be that much more extensive than the one from atop the saddle. Electric Peak (10,992 ft.) was named in 1872 by Henry Gannet of the Hayden party, who wrote of his July 26, 1872, climb of the peak: "A thunder-shower was approaching as we neared the summit of the mountain. I was above the others of the party, and, when about fifty feet below the summit, the electric current began to pass through my body. At first I felt nothing, but heard a crackling noise, similar to a rapid discharge of sparks from a friction machine. Immediately after, I began to feel a tingling, or prickling sensation in my head and the ends of my fingers, which as well as the noise, increased rapidly, until, when I reached the top, the noise, which had not changed its character, was deafening, and my hair stood completely on end, while the tingling, prickling sensation was absolutely painful. . . . We then returned down the mountain about three hundred feet, and to this point we still heard and felt the electricity."

As you begin your descent of the ridge, watch for animals—especially elk—grazing along the high, grassy slopes to the south. The Gardner River is crossed at 21.8 mi. mark. If you are planning to make a loop hike of Gallatin region, this is the spot to leave the trail. The Fawn Pass Trail is only 1 mi. to the south and can be joined by simply following the forest's edge south to Fawn Creek. If you continue on the Sportsman Lake Trail, you will reach the Cache Lake spur trail 1 mi. beyond the Gardner River; it is only 0.75 mi. up to the lake. From the east end of Cache Lake, there is a magnificent view of Electric Peak. There are no fish in Cache Lake, but it is ideal for duck and other waterbirds, and you may even spot a pair of trumpeter swan here.

From the Cache Lake spur trail the Sportsman Lake Trail continues down the headwaters of Glen Creek, crossing Snow Pass between Clagett Butte and Terrace Mountain at the 23.5 mi. mark. The old stage coach road from Mammoth used to cross this 7,450 ft. pass before the present

Kingman Pass (Golden Gate) Road was built. Only 1.5 mi. east of Snow Pass is the Mammoth-Norris Road.

High Lake Spur Trail   (3 mi.)

Start at Sportsman Lake Trail, 6.5 mi. from U.S. 191. From the Sportsman Lake Trail, it is a climb of about 750 ft. to High Lake, which sits at 8,774 ft., only 0.1 mi. inside the park boundary. Of the several alpine lakes in the northwest corner of the park, High Lake is popularly considered the most beautiful. Populations of cutthroat thrive here, but the fishing is rather poor. A U.S.F.S. trail along Mill Creek extends north from the High Lake area to the Cinnabar Basin, located in Gallatin National Forest.

Fawn Pass Trail   (21.5 mi.)

From the west, the trail begins from U.S. 191, 3 mi. north of Divide Lake. From the east, the trail begins from the Mammoth-Norris Road 2.5 mi. south of Mammoth. Snow Pass, which contains the old road used by stagecoaches before the present Kingman Pass (Golden Gate) Road was built, is crossed at 1.5 mi. From Glen Creek at the 2 mi. mark you cross Gardners Hole to the Gardner River, where you may spot big game, especially in early summer. Only 0.5 mi. beyond the Gardner River is Fawn Creek; both streams contain brook trout. As you enter the forest from Gardners Hole you will pass a meadow and pond. The trail then begins a gradual climb to Fawn Pass, following Fawn Creek most of the way to the top. About the 8 mi. mark you will be opposite a cirque to the south called the Pocket. A small lake is located there. Since much of the Gallatin Mountain Range between the Fawn Pass and Bighorn Pass trails is open, treeless country, you may want to consider some cross-country hiking between the 2 trails. Route-finding is easy, but you can expect to climb quite a bit. (Permission must be obtained in advance for off-trail travel.)

As you continue to gain elevation on the Fawn Pass Trail, you will begin to pass through more open areas which afford splendid views of the surrounding country. Gray Peak (10,292 ft.) is prominent to the north; its high grassy southern slopes are the summer home for a number of animals, particularly elk.

Fawn Pass provides an ideal habitat for the grizzly bear, and at times there is a rather large concentration of bears in the area. (A recent wildlife survey counted 22 bears within a 2 to 3 mi. radius of Fawn Pass.) There have also been a few recent encounters along the Fawn Pass and Bighorn Pass trails, which may eventually force the N.P.S. to restrict the use of the trails to parties of 4 or more. Bear incidents among large parties are very rare—they usually involve only 1 or 2 hikers. (A party of at least 3 is desirable so that in the event of injury, 1 person can stay with the injured hiker while the other goes for help.) A grizzly usually detects your presence with his incredibly sensitive nose. If the wind is not in your favor, then he may have to rely on his hearing to detect you. A grizzly's hearing is thought to be about equal to that of a man's, so if the wind is in your face and howling through the timber, a good loud pair of bear bells will prove to be most effective.

Evidence of bear activity can be seen at the Fawn Pass patrol cabin (the 11 mi. mark). The cabin is located to the south of the trail across Fawn Creek, and claw marks all around indicate that bears have tried to enter. You may also notice bear diggings and droppings along the way.

Atop the pass (9,100 ft.) is a small lake, which is the source for Fawn Creek. As you continue west from Fawn Pass the trail remains at a high elevation, affording fine views of the large meadows to the southwest. Along this stretch you will encounter dense patches of timber. At about the 14 mi. mark (8,200 ft.) there is a superb view to the southeast of Three Rivers Peak. The steep cirque above Gallatin Lake (the lake cannot be seen from here) usually contains snow throughout the summer. The forest below consists chiefly of spruce and fir.

At 16 mi. the Bighorn Pass Cutoff Trail permits a loop hike back on the Bighorn Pass Trail if desired. From this point, the trail continues through mostly open country. Many signs of bear are often noticeable along this stretch. At about the 18.5 mi. mark, several cold springs on both sides of the trail provide good drinking water. Fan Creek is reached at 19.5 mi. During 1974 a fire burned several hundred acres here. In order to reach U.S. 191, it is necessary to ford the Gallatin River. The vegetation surrounding the river consists of dense willow brush, which is good habitat for moose.

Bighorn Pass Trail   (20.3 mi.)

From the west, the trail begins at U.S. 191, 1 mi. north of Divide Lake. From the east, it begins at Indian Creek campground on the Mammoth-Norris Road, 8.5 mi. from Mammoth. From Indian Creek campground the trail crosses the southern tip of Gardners Hole and reaches Panther Creek at 4 mi. Johnson Gardner trapped beaver in this area as early as 1832. Another trapper, Osborne Russell, visited Gardners

Hole in 1839, according to his journals.

Panther Creek, which contains small brook and rainbow trout, is followed for most of the way to Bighorn Pass. The climb from Gardners Hole to Bighorn is 1,820 ft. As you begin the steep hike for the last 2 mi. up to Bighorn Pass, you will come on fine views of Bannock Peak to the north and Antler Peak to the south. (Bannock Peak and Indian Creek were named in honor of the tribe of Indians who inhabited the area to the southwest of the park.) The Great Bannock Trail passed near the Bighorn Pass Trail, following the valley of Indian Creek into Gardners Hole.

The valley below the Bighorn Pass Trail to the south contains several lakes (no fish). When above timberline around the pass, watch for bighorn sheep. Grizzlies are also common in this area, as at Fawn Pass. Atop Bighorn Pass (9,110 ft.) there are fine views to the east and west. One mi. south of Bighorn Pass (no trail) at 8,834 ft. is Gallatin Lake. Three Rivers Peak rises 1,122 ft. almost straight up from the lake. (The peak derives its name from the 3 streams—Gallatin River, Indian Creek, and Grayling Creek —that rise from its slopes.) From Bighorn Pass the trail descends sharply to the Gallatin River at the 10.7 mi. mark. The Gallatin River watershed contains brown and rainbow trout; both species were artificially introduced and have greatly displaced the native species of cutthroat and grayling. At 15.8 mi. is the cut-off trail which joins the Fawn Pass and Bighorn Pass trails, and which permits a loop hike if desired. From this point, the trail continues 4.5 mi. to U.S. 191, passing through more meadows along the way. It exits 1 mi. north of Divide Lake.

Beaver Ponds Loop Trail   (5 mi.)

Start from the old Mammoth-to-Gardiner dirt road. The
total distance for this trail is 5 mi., as it loops back to the
Mammoth area, exiting behind the U.S. Commissioner's
building (just north of Liberty Cap). The scenery consists
of a series of lakes set amid a forest of Douglas fir. The
distance can be shortened considerably by taking the old
Mammoth-to-Gardiner dirt road for about 1.5 mi., then
walking up the open ridge due west to join the trail. Once
here, you are only about 0.5 mi. from the lakes. Among the
Douglas fir are fields of wildflowers of all colors. Mule deer
are common in this area; you may also spot some antelope
in the open sagebrush country below you to the east. A
series of dams, constructed by beavers along the stream, has
resulted in several lakes at different levels. The beavers are
seldom seen during the day. They do most of their work in
the evening, beginning shortly before sundown.

Sepulcher Mountain Loop Trail   (10 mi.)

Start from behind the U.S. Commissioner's house (0.1 mi.
north of Liberty Cap). The trail climbs over 3,200 ft., making for a very strenuous trip, and one not highly recommended although from the summit (9,652 ft.) there are fine
views of Electric Peak, Gardners Hole, and the Mammoth
area. The peak was apparently named for a tomblike rock
(complete with prominent foot- and headstone) on the
northwest slope, which can be seen from the North Entrance. On the lower slopes is a large, light-colored deposit
of travertine, and hot springs which are currently active.
   Sepulcher Mountain is included in an interesting geologi-

cal structure, which consists of a downthrown block of the earth's crust. Some of the youngest known marine deposits in the park region are found here, as well as evidence of the earliest volcanic activity associated with the withdrawal of an ancient sea which once covered this region. From the summit you may choose to descend the mountain the same way, or complete the loop by descending to Snow Pass and exiting on the Mammoth-Norris Road, 2.5 mi. north of Mammoth. The distance is about the same either way.

Mt. Holmes Trail   (10.8 mi.)

The trailhead is on the west side of the Mammoth-Norris Road (0.3 mi. south of Apollinaris Springs). The climb of 3,000 ft. to the summit of Mt. Holmes is strenuous, but once on top you will have magnificent views of the surrounding country. At the 2.7 mi. mark you reach the Grizzly Lake Trail, which leads 1.5 mi. south to the lake. Continuing on the right fork, you will reach a meadow at the 5.5 mi. mark. At the west end of this meadow you come to the junction of the Cougar Creek Trail. The trail really begins to climb sharply from this point, gaining about 2,500 ft. in the last 4 mi. to the summit. Timberline is reached at the saddle between White Peaks and Mt. Holmes. Below you to the northwest is the source of Indian Creek.

Mt. Holmes (10,336 ft.) was named in 1878 for W. F. Holmes, a geologist with the U.S. Geological Survey. The views from the summit on a clear day take in most of the park's prominent features. A fire lookout is stationed here for most of the summer.

Grizzly Lake Trail   (1.7 mi.)

This particular trail is rather new and not shown on present U.S.G.S. topo maps. It begins from the wide loop in the road about 1 mi. south of Beaver Lake, then crosses a marshy area which sometimes contains moose. You will not be able to see the lake until you are 300 yds. from its shores, as it lies deep in a narrow timbered valley. When you do see it, you will be about 350 ft. above, and will command a splendid view, with Mt. Holmes as an impressive backdrop. The trail descends to the north end of the lake.

Cougar Creek Trail   (21.5 mi.)

Start out from the Mt. Holmes Trail at the 5.8 mi. mark. From the Mt. Holmes Trail all the way to Cougar Creek patrol cabin, the trail winds through a lodgepole forest with no openings, providing rather monotonous scenery. So, unless this trail is being used to gain access to the Gallatin area, it is not recommended.

Gneiss Creek Trail   (14 mi.)

The trailhead is on the north side of the West Entrance Road, 4 mi. from the entrance station. The trail passes through many openings and meadows, and crosses several streams. The region traversed by this trail is known as the Madison Valley or Baker's Hole. Chances are you will not see another soul along the way. There are excellent opportunities for the fishing enthusiast.

At the 2 mi. mark you will cross an old dirt road which leads over to the Madison River 4 mi. away, then follows its east shore for several miles. Grizzlies often inhabit the Madison Valley, particularly the open meadows along Cougar Creek, so be sure to remain alert and make noise as you hike.

From Cougar Creek the trail passes through many meadows and openings the rest of the way. At 7.7 mi. Maple Creek is crossed. Gneiss Creek is reached in a large meadow at 9.5 mi., then Campanula Creek at 12 mi. For an interesting side trip, you should follow the unnamed stream just west of Campanula Creek south for about 1 mi. to a large meadow where Gneiss, Campanula, and Richards creeks combine to form Duck Creek. Watch for elk in this vicinity, and also sandhill crane near the mouth of Richards Creek. The trail continues for 2 more miles until it exits at U.S. 191, 9 mi. north of West Yellowstone.

Monument Geyser Basin Trail   (1 mi.)

The starting point for this trail is on the west side of the Norris-Madison Road, 5 mi. south of Norris (at the bridge). The trail follows the Madison River upstream for 0.5 mi., then climbs 700 ft. in the next 0.5 mi. This thermal region was discovered by Park Superintendent P. W. Norris in 1878. Monument Geyser usually has a small spray of water erupting from its 8 ft. cylindrical cone. Several other smaller cones grouped nearby are now dormant. A boiling sulphur caldron and some steam vents are also located in this group.

To the north of Monument Geyser Basin on the base of the ridge is the Sylvan Springs group, which can easily be viewed across the Gibbon Meadows from the road. It contains steam vents, mudpots, and a large mud caldron formed as a result of the 1959 earthquake. You can reach this area by walking along the southern edge of the Gibbon Meadows (avoiding the wet, marshy meadow itself), but the thermal regions here contain thin crusts in some areas, so be extremely cautious.

Purple Mountain Lookout Trail   (3.3 mi.)

Begin from the north side of the Madison-Norris Road, 0.7 mi. from Madison Junction. A climb of 1,600 ft. through the forest brings you to the summit. Along the way you will see the evidence of forest fires in the vicinity.

At 1.5 mi. you may notice an old sign dating back perhaps 35 years: "Yellowstone Trail Located by Hugh Peyton." At 1.8 mi. and for the remainder of the hike to the summit there are distant views through the trees: The Terrace Spring area, the stream from the Fountain Paint Pots area, and Midway Geyser Basin (to the right of Fountain Paint Pots) can all be seen. As you approach the summit at the 3.3 mi. mark, the views of the entire Madison area—including Madison Canyon, National Park Mountain, and the junction of the Gibbon and Firehole rivers—become more spectacular. It was at this junction below what is now known as National Park Mountain that members of the 1870 Washburn Expedition sat around a campfire on the evening of September 19, 1870, and discussed the marvels they had just discovered.

On a clear day you will be able to see parts of the Beartooth Range, the Absaroka Range, Mt. Washburn, and the Teton Range. Take binoculars on this trip.

Harlequin Lake Trail   (0.5 mi.)

The trail begins 1.7 mi. from Madison Junction on the north side of the West Entrance Road. This short path winds through dense lodgepole to the lake (actually just a lilypad pond). Purple Mountain (8,433 ft.) rises to the northeast. No fish live in this small body of water, but there are usually duck.

Osprey Falls (150 ft.)

Washburn Region

This wilderness region contains very few trails, but there are some good cross-country hikes. Three major streams—Blacktail Deer, Lava, and Tower creeks—originate at the foot of the Washburn Range and flow north to the Yellowstone River. The Washburn Range is actually the upper portion of a much more extensive mountain range, which was covered by lava flows millions of years ago.

The trails described in this section exist only along the perimeters of the Washburn region. Special permission must be obtained for those experienced hikers who wish to traverse the region without the benefit of trails.

Most of the area is heavily forested with lodgepole pine, with the exception of the Blacktail Deer Plateau. The dense lodgepole growth is quite evident when driving from Norris to Canyon, and also from atop Dunraven Pass.

WASHBURN REGION TRAILS

Cascade Lake Picnic Area to Beaver Lake . . . . 18 mi.

Osprey Falls Trail . . . . 2 mi.

Bunsen Peak Trail . . . . 5 mi.

Wraith Falls Trail . . . . 0.25 mi.

Lost Falls Trail . . . . 0.25 mi.

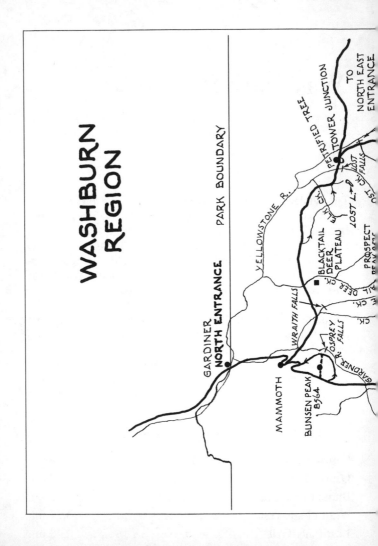

WASHBURN REGION

PARK BOUNDARY

YELLOWSTONE R.

GARDINER
NORTH ENTRANCE

PETRIFIED TREE

TOWER JUNCTION

TO
NORTH EAST
ENTRANCE

LOST CR. LOST
FALLS

LOST L.

BLACKTAIL
DEER
PLATEAU

PROSPECT
PEAK

ELK CR.

DEER CR.

WRAITH FALLS

MAMMOTH

OSPREY FALLS

GARDNER R.

BUNSEN PEAK
8564

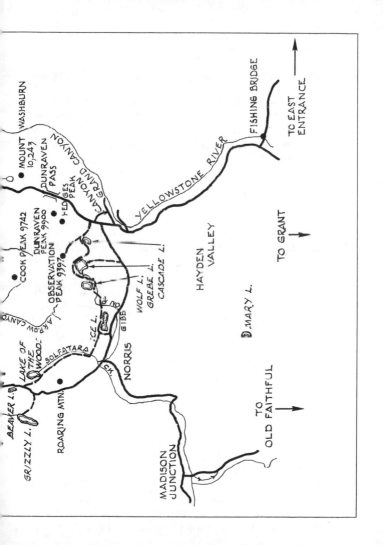

Cascade Lake Picnic Area to Beaver Lake   (18 mi.)

Start from the trailhead at the picnic area, 1.25 mi. north of Canyon Junction on the Canyon-Tower Road. However, this hike may be varied considerably by joining the trail at other locations, taking either the Cascade Lake, Grebe Lake, or Ice Lake trails. Although the trail is marked, parts are not maintained due to a revision of the trail system. The trail passes through forest, meadow, and marshland to Cascade and Grebe lakes. In early summer there are occasionally a few grizzlies in this area, but they generally move on as the summer progresses. Separate trails lead into both Cascade and Grebe lakes. A spur trail leads to the top of Observation Peak (9,397 ft.). This trail, which is 3 mi. long and not shown on most maps, begins just east of Cascade Lake and climbs 1,400 ft. to the top. The view of Grebe Lake, the heavily forested Solfatara Plateau, and the Canyon area is magnificent.

Wolf Lake is almost surrounded by meadows and is an excellent area for deer, moose, and elk. There are arctic grayling and rainbow in the lake. (Grayling are quite rare in Yellowstone and found mainly in Ice, Wolf, and Grebe lakes; catch-and-release regulation is in effect—none may be kept.) From Wolf Lake to Ice Lake the trail continues through dense lodgepole, crossing the Gibbon River several times. Ice Lake is completely surrounded by lodgepole; there are no meadows along the shores. The most beautiful view is at sunrise from the western shore. This lake reportedly holds a population of grayling; the park's last artificial stocking of fish took place here in 1961, when 10,000 grayling fry were released. However, the fishing here is poor— perhaps because Ice Lake does not have a permanent inlet or outlet. There are almost always a number of duck on the lake, but the more elegant trumpeter swan usually picks Grebe Lake for a summer home. (Ice Lake can also be reached by a short 0.25-mi. trail from the Norris-Canyon Road.)

At 15 mi. Solfatara Creek is reached. Norris campground and Ranger Station are only 1 mi. downstream. The upper reaches of Solfatara Creek contain a number of small brook trout. Extensive meadows appear near the headwaters of the creek at the 14.5 mi. mark. Lake of the Woods, at 17 mi., lies amid dense lodgepole. Reports in the late 1880's told of fish here, but currently there are none. Just southeast of Lake of the Woods is a solfataric area and a large hot spring—Amphitheater Springs—which is the source for Lemonade Creek. Indians used the substantial amounts of vermilion in the springs area for paint. From Lake of the Woods the trail (which is poorly marked) follows Lemonade Creek down to the Mammoth-Norris Road and emerges just south of Beaver Lake.

Osprey Falls Trail (2 mi.)

Start from the trailhead off the Bunsen Peak Loop Road, a 6 mi., one-way dirt road beginning from the Mammoth-Norris Road (east side) 0.2 mi. south of Rustic Falls and the Golden Gate (5 mi. from Mammoth). The road is narrow and mostly downhill. It is closed at dark and also when conditions are unsafe. The trailhead, which should be marked, is on the right side of the road, about 3 mi. along. This trip is often overlooked, but offers some of the most spectacular scenery available in the park for such a short distance. The trail follows a series of switchbacks to the bottom of the very impressive 800 ft. deep Sheepeater Canyon, through which the Gardner River flows. The Sheepeater Canyon, with Osprey Falls at its head, ranks second only to the Grand Canyon of Yellowstone as the park's most impressive canyon. As you begin your descent, Sheepeater Cliffs across the gorge will come into full view. These cliffs were named by P. W. Norris for the Sheepeater Indians, a small band of poor and crudely equipped people who occupied this area of the park. Bighorn sheep are occasionally spotted along the cliff's rims. The canyon has been carved into the durable volcanic rock through countless ages, mostly by stream and glacial erosion. At the bottom the trail parallels the raging Gardner River. Osprey Falls (150 ft.) is hidden from view until the last possible moment due to a rise in the trail; the magnificent cataract bursts into view on crossing this small hill. It is impossible to climb up to the brink without extreme danger. The only other feasible view of Osprey Falls (but from a mile off) is obtained from the Bunsen Peak Loop Road.

Bunsen Peak Trail   (5 mi.)

Start from the Bunsen Peak Loop Road, 0.2 mi. south of Rustic Falls and the Golden Gate (5 mi. from Mammoth). The summit of Bunsen Peak is 1,345 ft. higher than the road. There is a small TV tower on top. Bunsen Peak was named for the eminent physicist and chemist, Robert W. Bunsen, who invented the Bunsen burner, and who was first to thoroughly investigate the phenomenon of geysers. From the summit there is a magnificent view of Gardners Hole, including Swan Lake Flat, the Mammoth area, and Electric Peak. In 1872, E. S. Topping and D. Woodruff discovered

Norris Geyser Basin from this summit, as they spotted large columns of steam rising far to the south.

Wraith Falls Trail   (0.25 mi.)

The south side of Mammoth-Tower Road, 5 mi. from Mammoth, is the starting point for this walk. It begins in a meadow, but enters a thick forest consisting of lodgepole, spruce, and fir near the foot of the falls. Wraith Falls is actually a cascade about 80 ft. high. The scenery is delightful, with Lupine Creek rushing over boulders amid rich forest undergrowth.

Lost Falls Trail   (0.25 mi.)

This short walk begins directly behind Roosevelt Lodge. From Roosevelt Lodge, follow Lost Creek upstream to the foot of the falls in a steep timber-covered canyon. Lost Falls plunges 40 ft. over the canyon's edge. Two-tenths of a mile west of the falls is Lost Lake.

Trout Lake

North of Yellowstone River Region

This wilderness region is the smallest of the 7 backcountry areas included in this book. However, it borders the 64,000 acre Absaroka Primitive Area to the north, so the continuous wilderness is quite extensive. Elevations range from 5,500 ft. along the Yellowstone River to over 9,200 ft. on the Buffalo Plateau along the northern boundary, and 10,638 ft. atop Cutoff Peak in the northeastern section. The mountain scenery in the northeast section is extremely rugged, comparable to that of Glacier National Park in northern Montana.

Although there are a number of connecting trails, 3 extensive backcountry trips are available in this region. One begins from Gardiner or Blacktail Deer Creek and follows the Yellowstone River to Hellroaring Creek. The second takes the Buffalo Plateau Trail, which begins from near Hellroaring Creek, loops into the Absaroka Primitive Area, and ends at Slough Creek. The third possibility is to hike up Slough Creek, take the Elk Tongue Creek Trail over Bliss Pass, then the Pebble Creek Trail downstream to Pebble Creek campground or upstream to near the Northeast Entrance—both on the Northeast Entrance Road.

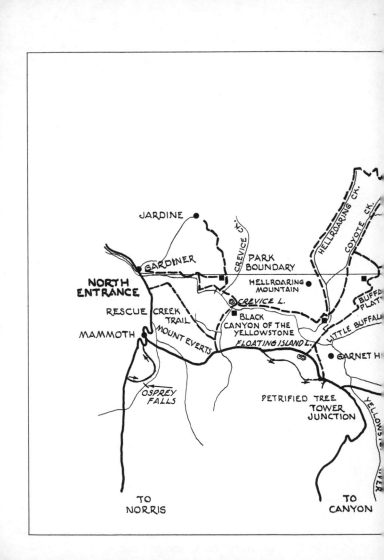

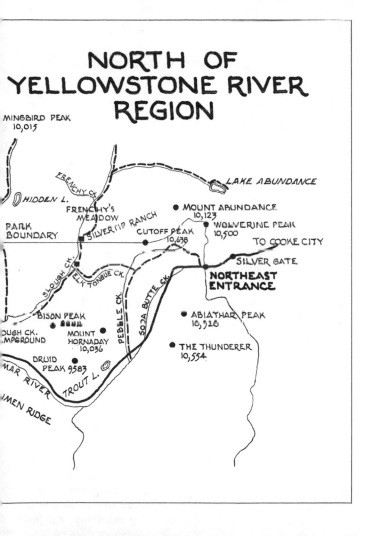

NORTH OF YELLOWSTONE RIVER REGION

MINGBIRD PEAK
10,015

FRENCHY CK.

LAKE ABUNDANCE

HIDDEN L.

FRENCHY'S MEADOW

SILVER TIP RANCH

MOUNT ABUNDANCE
10,123

WOLVERINE PEAK
10,500

PARK BOUNDARY

CUTOFF PEAK
10,638

TO COOKE CITY

SILVER GATE

SLOUGH CK.

ELK TONGUE CK.

SODA BUTTE CK.

PEBBLE CK.

NORTHEAST ENTRANCE

BISON PEAK

SLOUGH CK. CAMPGROUND

MOUNT HORNADAY
10,036

ABIATHAR PEAK
10,928

DRUID PEAK 9583

TROUT L.

THE THUNDERER
10,554

LAMAR RIVER

SPECIMEN RIDGE

NORTH OF YELLOWSTONE
RIVER REGION TRAILS

Yellowstone River Trail
    (Gardiner to Hellroaring Creek) . . . . 14.5 mi.

Rescue Creek Trail
    (Mammoth-Tower Road to Gardner River) . . . . . . 8 mi.

Lower Blacktail Trail
    (Mammoth-Tower Road to Yellowstone River) . . . 4 mi.

Hellroaring Creek Trail
    (Mammoth-Tower Road to Northern Boundary) . . 7 mi.

Buffalo Plateau Trail
    (Mammoth-Tower Road to Slough Creek) . . . . . 21 mi.

Slough Creek Trail
    (Slough Creek Campground to Northern Boundary) 11 mi.

Slough Creek to Northeast Entrance Road (via Elk
    Tongue Creek and Pebble Creek Trails) . . . 11.5, 13 mi.

Trout Lake Trail . . . . 0.3 mi.

Yellowstone River Trail
(Gardiner to Hellroaring Creek)   (14.5 mi.)

The trail begins just north of the Yellowstone River Bridge
in Gardiner, Montana (immediately opposite the first service station on the north side of the bridge). The trail from
Gardiner along the Yellowstone River is not very scenic for
the first 6 mi. as it runs through an extremely dry area with
very little vegetation. The best plan is to take the Lower
Blacktail Trail down to the river, the continue upstream to
Hellroaring Creek. This trail begins from the north side of
the Mammoth-Tower Road, 7 mi. from Mammoth and just

west of Blacktail Deer Creek. The hike along the Yellowstone River is quite hot most of the summer, due to the low elevation and dry conditions, but it is certainly the ideal trip in spring, early summer and late fall (when most of the park's trails at higher elevations are snowed in). In early spring, look for bighorn, elk, deer, and antelope. In late autumn, when the first heavy snows begin to fall, deer and elk begin their migration down from atop the plateau to the Yellowstone River in search of available forage.

The first interesting scenery begins as you approach Knowles Falls, a 15 ft. drop of the Yellowstone River. When the water is down late in the summer, and conditions are right (e.g., during the stonefly hatch), fly fishing on the Yellowstone River for large cutthroat is at its peak. The vicinity at the foot of Knowles Falls is excellent, but be careful since access is difficult here. At Knowles Falls you will be in the heart of the Black Canyon, so named for the dark-shaded canyon walls rising above the river. As you hike from the falls up to Crevice Lake you pass through what amounts to an animal graveyard. Along this 1 mi. stretch you will notice many bones, antlers, and skulls—chiefly elk—but also perhaps a few deer or bighorn. Hundreds of elk winter in this area each year, and sometimes there is simply not enough food for all. This natural process of winterkill helps control the populations, especially elk. Crevice Creek is crossed 0.5 mi. upstream from Knowles Falls; there is a short spur trail which leads up to the park boundary. In 1867, prospectors discovered gold up this creek and also up Bear Creek (the trail crosses it 2 mi. from Gardiner) outside the park.

Crevice Lake at the 7.5 mi. mark has no inlet or outlet and sits in a deeply depressed bowl. There are no fish. The trail passes high above the lake on its northeastern side, with a fine view of the Black Canyon in the background. A short distance beyond the lake the trail reaches Blacktail bridge, a suspension bridge which provides access to the Lower Blacktail Trail leading to the Mammoth-Tower Road.

The Yellowstone River Trail continues along the north side of the river. After crossing Cottonwood Creek at the 10.5 mi. mark, it begins to turn from the river and leads through open sagebrush to Hellroaring Creek. There is a footbridge across the creek 0.5 mi. upstream from Hellroaring Creek patrol cabin. From here it is 3.5 mi. up to the Mammoth-Tower Road near Floating Island Lake.

Rescue Creek Trail
(Mammoth-Tower Road to Gardner River)   (8 mi.)

The trailhead is on the north side of the Mammoth-Tower Road, 7 mi. from Mammoth, west of Blacktail Deer Creek. This trail chiefly traverses open sagebrush and is interesting during spring and fall as the wildlife-viewing opportunities are good, especially for antelope; however, during the summer the trip is hot and dry. There are several ponds along the way whose origins trace back to large glacial lakes formed by retreating glaciers. There are usually various waterbirds on the lakes.

Truman Everts was supposedly found at Rescue Creek on October 16, 1870, after 37 days of wandering in Yellowstone's wilderness. Actually, Everts was found about 2 mi. up the eastern fork of Blacktail Deer Creek (south of the Mammoth-Tower Road). He was in critical condition, but eventually recovered to live to the age of 85.

At 5 mi. Rattlesnake Butte appears to the north. (There are no poisonous snakes in Yellowstone, with the exception of the lower elevations in this area, where an occasional rattler is found.) The trail crosses the Gardner River (bridge provided) and joins the road 0.7 mi. from the North Entrance. Less than 1 mi. south of this point is MacMinn Bench, on the lower slopes of Everts Mountain. From October to June, this area contains fascinating wildlife. During early morning and late afternoon you may expect to see herds of bighorn sheep, antelope, deer, and elk grazing on the slopes, with an occasional coyote checking the edges of the herds for a weak specimen. Access to the slopes of the bench is easily gained from the Gardner River footbridge.

Lower Blacktail Trail
(Mammoth-Tower Road to Yellowstone River)   (4 mi.)

Start out from the same trailhead as Rescue Creek Trail. This hike is quite popular as it provides access to a beautiful area in the Black Canyon. The trail passes through open sagebrush and descends over 1,000 ft. to the river, which makes for a rough return trip on a hot summer day. Soils here are glacial till, deep and well drained; as a result, there is little surface moisture. On the way down to the river you may spot deer, antelope, and even an occasional bighorn sheep. During May and June, elk often calve in this area while traveling from their low-lying winter range to the high plateau country. Blacktail Bridge affords access across the Yellowstone River, and to such attractions as Knowles Falls, Crevice Lake, and the Black Canyon.

Hellroaring Creek Trail
## (Mammoth-Tower Road to Northern Boundary)					(7 mi.)

The trail begins on the north side of the Mammoth-Tower Road, 3.3 mi. from Tower and just north of Floating Island Lake. Most maps do not show this trailhead; it affords a shorter trip down to the Yellowstone River, as compared to beginning from Lost Creek or Elk Creek. The trail descends some 750 ft. in 1 mi. to the Yellowstone River, passing Garnet Hill on the east. Garnet Hill is composed of ancient granitic gneiss over a billion years old. A suspension bridge crosses the Yellowstone River at a point where it rushes through a deep gorge. After passing the Buffalo Plateau Trail junction in open sagebrush, you will see ponds of glacial origin where there are almost always some duck.

At the 3 mi. mark you reach Hellroaring Creek, with the patrol cabin across stream. Gold prospectors along the Yellowstone River in 1867 described this creek as a "real hell roarer," and the name stuck. (A footbridge across Hellroaring Creek is provided 0.5 mi. upstream from the cabin.) The creek contains a population of cutthroat trout; however, high waters often persist through mid-July.

The prominent cone-shaped mountain to the northwest is Hellroaring Mountain, one of the park's few granite peaks not covered by volcanic lava flows of the Tertiary period. From the Hellroaring Creek patrol cabin area you have several choices: you may follow the creek up into the Absaroka Primitive Area; you may do the same by following Coyote Creek Trail; or you may angle up the ridge in a northeasterly direction until you join the Buffalo Plateau Trail, which is the only feasible hike if you plan to loop back down in the park. If you continue north along Hell-

roaring Creek across the boundary, lakes, waterfalls, mountains, forest, and meadows await you in the Absaroka Primitive Area of Gallatin National Forest. (A Montana State
fishing license is required if you plan to do any fishing.)

Buffalo Plateau Trail
(Mammoth-Tower Road to Slough Creek)   (21 mi.)

Set out from the same trailhead as Hellroaring Creek Trail.
A complete hike of the Buffalo Plateau Trail ranks as one
of the finest available in the park; the scenery is wild and
quite varied. The Buffalo Plateau Trail begins 0.4 mi. north
of the suspension bridge over the Yellowstone River, however, a good plan is to camp on Hellroaring Creek (across
from the patrol cabin) and then join the Buffalo Plateau
Trail by angling up the open slopes in a northeasterly direction. Otherwise it is a long, hard climb of 3,000 ft. up to
the plateau, and unless you get a very early start, you may
not make it to the Buffalo Fork Creek in the Absaroka
Primitive Area, which is by far the best available camping
spot. If you do decide on this plan, be certain to cross over
the Coyote Creek Trail to the Buffalo Plateau Trail and not
go up Coyote Creek by mistake.

A trip on the Buffalo Plateau requires a 15-min. topo
map of Mt. Wallace, Montana, since the trail crosses over
the park boundary. If camping on Hellroaring Creek, be
sure to take a good look at the summit of Hellroaring
Mountain high above you, for when you reach the top of
the plateau, it will be far *below* you. The trail climbs steadily through open sagebrush to the top, providing wide vistas
of the surrounding countryside. Herds of antelope are common. The prominent skyline of the Gallatin Range lies to

the west and the Washburn Range to the south. Peaks are easily identified by referring to your topo maps, especially Electric Peak, Mt. Holmes, and Mt. Washburn. As you climb higher you will begin to enter patches of forest, with Douglas fir predominating. The trail becomes difficult to follow over open areas, so look closely for the orange trail markers. When you reach Buffalo patrol cabin, you will have climbed to near the 9,000 ft. mark. (The cabin is usually occupied during the fall hunting season to ensure against hunters accidentally crossing over the boundary.) The next mile beyond the cabin passes through superb subalpine scenery, with the rugged Beartooth Range to the north. When the boundary is crossed, you will note a steep rise to your left that contains a trail—*do not take this*; rather, continue due north until you reach the U.S.F.S. Buffalo Plateau Trail, which extends west-east and is well marked all the way to Buffalo Fork Creek. In the early 1900's, this trail was maintained by poachers, but it is now official, though some signs still refer to it as "Poacher's Trail."

When you have descended nearly 2,000 ft. from the plateau down to Buffalo Fork Creek, you emerge into a meadow which is a fine place to camp. The creek provides excellent fishing for small but tasty rainbow trout. Hummingbird Peak (over 10,000 ft.) provides a beautiful background. If you decide to spend an extra day here, you may want to explore the trail to the north, up the Buffalo Fork Creek for about 3 mi., where you enter another extensive meadow. Half a mile east of the trail (across the creek) is Hidden Lake, which as its name suggests, lies hidden between a small hill and the side of a mountain. The lake covers about 10 acres and is quite deep, with talus slopes extending to the water at the southeast end. Remember, a

Montana fishing license is required for waters north of the park

The Buffalo Plateau Trail crosses Buffalo Fork Creek, then follows the meadow around to its southeast end (away from the creek), where it continues mostly through timber and high on the ridge above Buffalo Creek, before emerging into a large, open area containing groves of aspen. (Many of the trees show scar rings caused by the continuous rubbing of elk antlers on the bark.) From the edge of the plateau in this open country you can see Slough Creek Valley below and craggy Cutoff Peak (10,638 ft.) to the northeast. If you have binoculars, scan the valley below you for wildlife—especially moose, elk, and the occasional coyote. You must ford Slough Creek. (Note that the creek can be treacherous in early summer during high water, and this particular ford is not recommended until the water level goes down in mid-July). The trail then joins an old wagon road leading to Slough Creek campground, 2 mi. away.

Slough Creek Trail
(Slough Creek Campground to Northern Boundary)(11 mi.)

The starting point is Slough Creek campground, reached by a dirt road from the Tower-Northeast Entrance Road. Beautiful scenery, with views of rugged peaks, and fine aspen groves await those who travel up Slough Creek. After 2 mi. the trail breaks into Slough Creek Valley. Watch here for moose, elk, and deer. Cutoff Peak dominates the view at the head of the Slough Creek Valley. In 1867 a gold prospector, when asked by a traveling party about this stream, described it as "but a slough." However, when the party reached the creek they encountered a rushing torrent and lost a fully loaded pack horse while crossing it. Generally

speaking, the fishing for Slough Creek's cutthroat trout im-
proves as you work your way upstream. (Remember, current fishing regulations must be observed.)

Rather than continue on the old wagon road, you do
better to take a detour by McBride Lake. This is done by
crossing the creek following the Buffalo Plateau Trail, then
veering eastward across the meadows to the lake, which is
hidden among timber and perpendicular rock walls. However, this detour should be attempted only after mid-July
when the ford of Slough Creek may be safely accomplished.
McBride Lake is probably Yellowstone's most beautiful
backcountry lake. The lake contains populations of cutthroat
trout; however, remember that these waters are catch and
release waters only. The lake receives quite a bit of day-use
fishing. Overnight camping is not allowed. The majority of
today's backpackers are responsible hikers, but the day-use
fisherman is often guilty of littering the area.

Following the lake's northwestern shore, you will pass a
meadow at the north end through which an inlet flows to
the lake. Moose are often seen here. The wagon road may
be rejoined by veering south and crossing Slough Creek.
There is a large aspen grove on the ridge south of the road
near Plateau Creek.

At the confluence of Slough and Elk Tongue creeks, the
8 mi. mark, some good campsites are located. From here the
Elk Tongue Creek Trail begins its climb of 2,600 ft. up to
Bliss Pass. If you continue upstream along Slough Creek,
you will come upon the Silvertip Ranch, just north of the
park boundary. During the early 1900's, Frenchy Duret, a
man of French-Canadian descent lived here. He maintained
a small herd of cattle which he often illegally allowed to
graze inside the park. Duret was also a noted poacher of

park game, but although rangers tried to catch him in the act, he always managed to elude them. Rumor had it that he harbored a particular hatred for grizzlies, since his pet dogs had been killed by one. One summer's morning in 1922 Duret discovered a huge grizzly caught in one of his steel bear traps. He returned to his cabin, retrieved his rifle, and proceeded to shoot the bear. Apparently he did not strike a vital spot, for the bear lunged forward and broke free from the trap, falling on Duret and wounding him severely; the grizzly then left the scene. Duret, upon regaining consciousness, began a slow crawl back to his cabin, 0.75 mi. away. He made it to the edge of his property, then died under his own fence. Frenchy Duret was buried near his cabin. His gravestone, near the Silvertip Ranch, reads "Joseph Duret, Born in France 1858, Died 1922."

The bear, whose bloody trail led down Slough Creek, was never found. Newspaper clippings and a 1922 letter from Horace Albright—then the park's superintendent—which discuss the fruitless search for the grizzly are posted in the lobby of the Silvertip Ranch. According to Albright, it left behind the largest set of tracks he had ever seen in Yellowstone. Presumably, offspring of this bear inhabit Yellowstone Park today. Three miles north of Silvertip Ranch is Frenchy's Meadow.

Slough Creek to Northeast Entrance Road (via Elk Tongue Creek and Pebble Creek Trails)   (11.5, 13 mi.)

The trail starts out from near the confluence of Slough and Elk Tongue creeks on the old wagon road 8 mi. from Slough Creek campground; however, if you wish to start at the other end of the hike, you may begin on the Pebble

Creek Trail at Pebble Creek campground, 9.5 mi. from the Northeast Entrance, or the trailhead 1.2 mi. inside the Northeast Entrance. It is a hard 4 mi. up Elk Tongue Creek to Bliss Pass, as you climb over 2,600 ft., mostly through timber. When you near Bliss Pass, you will pass a small pond on your right (SE); at this point be sure to climb the small ridge to your left (NW) for a fine view of the Slough Creek Valley, which you cannot see from the pass itself. The Bliss Pass vicinity is good habitat for bear, so make noise and be alert. At the actual summit of the pass there is a good view of the rugged peaks to the northeast. The large meadow to the northeast contains the north Pebble Creek Trail which exits near the Northeast Entrance. From Bliss Pass down to Pebble Creek and out to the road, the trail passes through spectacular mountain scenery which is among the best Yellowstone has to offer.

The trail drops practically straight down to Pebble Creek on a series of switchbacks. At Pebble Creek you reach one of the most beautiful campsites in Yellowstone Park, yet it is seldom used. Here you come to a stream with cutthroat trout. If you continue south on the Pebble Creek Trail, you will pass under Baronette Peak (10,404 ft.) to the east and Mt. Hornaday (10,036 ft.) to the west, before reaching Pebble Creek campground 7.5 mi. away. The more scenic trip, and also the shorter trip to the road, is made by continuing up the Pebble Creek Trail, which bends around to the east and exits near the Northeast Entrance. The trail passes through spruce and fir for 2 mi. before entering the large meadow which is visible from Bliss Pass. The fishing is still good this far upstream, although mostly for smaller sizes. The trail leaves Pebble Creek and makes a short climb up to the saddle in the ridge, then begins a descent of about

1,000 ft. to the Northeast Entrance Road. The views of Abiathar Park (10,928 ft.) across the way, and of the valley through which Soda Butte Creek courses, are spectacular. The trail reaches the road 1.2 mi. from the Northeast Entrance. For a wonderful short trip which provides spectacular scenery, the 1.5 mi. hike from here over the saddle down to Pebble Creek cannot be topped.

Trout Lake Trail   (0.3 mi.)

Start from the Tower-Northeast Entrance Road, 12.7 mi. from the Northeast Entrance (about 1.8 mi. south of Pebble Creek campground). The trail is not marked by a sign. This is a very good short trip, whether you plan to fish or not. The trail climbs sharply over a small ridge which for most of the way is carpeted with wildflowers. At the top of the hill you reach a huge Douglas fir; from here you have good views of The Thunderer (10,554 ft.) to the east and Mt. Hornaday (10,036 ft.) to the north. Trout Lake is surrounded by meadows to the west and north. You may notice an artificial spillway at the lake's outlet which was constructed in conjunction with the fish hatchery once operated here. The lake is quite deep and contains mostly whopper-sized rainbow trout, which are not easy to catch. Nearby Buck and Shrimp lakes contain few, if any, fish.

Fern Lake

Mirror Plateau Region

The Mirror plateau wilderness area is very large and contains some of the wildest and most interesting backcountry scenery to be found in Yellowstone. There are extensive thermal areas, fossil forests, a portion of the Grand Canyon of Yellowstone, rugged mountain scenery, fine meadows and valleys, and abundant wildlife.

Under an experimental forest fire management program, the National Park Service has designated the heavily forested backcountry of the Mirror Plateau, along with the Two Ocean Plateau, as areas where *natural* forest fires will be allowed to burn without man's interference, though under close observation. Most of the trails within this region are in very poor condition because of high water during the spring run-off. For this reason it is best to plan your longer trips for no earlier than July 1.

MIRROR PLATEAU REGION TRAILS

Lamar River Trail (and Side
    Trips From Cold Creek Junction) . . . . 17.5 mi.
The Thunderer Cutoff Trail . . . . 7.5 mi.
Cache Creek Trail . . . . 16.6 mi.

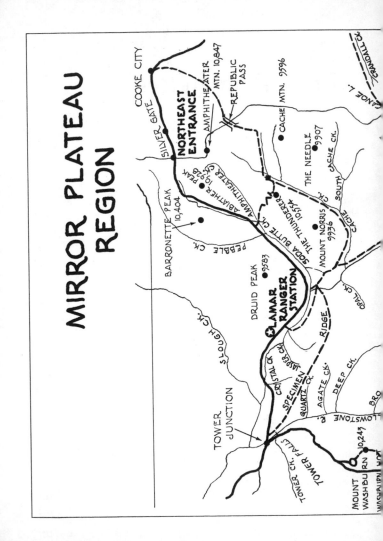

MIRROR PLATEAU REGION

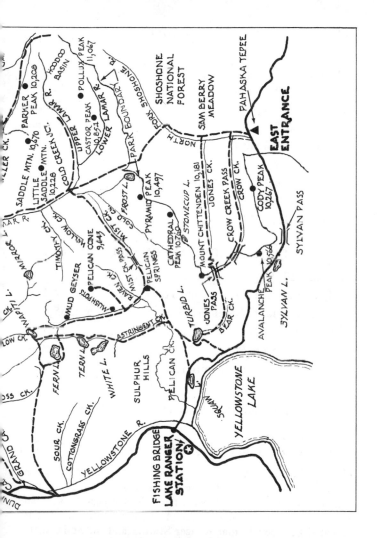

Miller Creek Trail (and Side
Trips From Upper Miller Creek) . . . . .8.5 mi.

Specimen Ridge Trail . . . . 17.5 mi.

Wapiti Lake Trail . . . . 14.5 mi.

Mt. Washburn Trail . . . . 3 mi.

Tower Falls Trail . . . . .0.4 mi.

Pelican Creek-Astringent Creek Loop Trail . . 16.5, 11 mi.

Jones Pass-Crow Creek Pass Trail . . . . 13 mi.

Avalanche Peak Hike . . . . 2 mi.

SHORT HIKES FROM CANYON VILLAGE AREA

Crystal Falls-Upper Falls Trail . . . . .0.6 mi.

Ribbon Lake-Clear Lake Loop Trail . . . . .4.2 mi.

Glacial Boulder to Seven-Mile Hole . . . . .5.1 mi.

Grebe Lake Trail . . . . 3 mi.

Cascade Lake Trail . . . . .2.8 mi.

Glacial Boulder to Washburn Hot Springs . . . . 4 mi.

MIRROR PLATEAU REGION TRAILS

Lamar River Trail
(and Side Trips From Cold Creek Junction)   (17.5 mi.)

The trailhead is on the Tower Junction-Northeast Entrance
Road, 15 mi. east of Tower Junction (4.3 mi. east of the
Lamar Ranger Station), which provides access to a small
bridge across Soda Butte Creek. There are 2 other trailheads
located between Lamar Ranger Station and the Soda Butte

Trailhead for horse parties. The first 3.5 mi. traverse a large meadow in the Lamar Valley and lead down to Cache Creek. Along the way there are several stands of aspen. Aspens in Yellowstone have been on a steady decline. This is believed to be the result of winter overgrazing by elk, and also the lack of forest fires which, as in the case of the lodgepole pine, play an instrumental role in the reproduction of the species.

At the 3.3 mi. mark you come to a trail junction where the Cache Creek Trail forks to the east; from this junction, the Lamar River Trail descends sharply to Cache Creek. Cache Creek derives its name from a prospecting party in 1863 which was surprised by Indians while camped on the creek. All their stock was lost or stolen except for a few mules, and as a result the party was forced to "cache" much of their gear at this location and pick it up later. Unfortunately for the backpacker there is no bridge across the icy waters of the creek. *This crossing is not recommended before July 1*, due to very high water.

The trail from Cache Creek to Cold Creek Junction contains very little change of scenery, as it follows the Lamar River through mostly wooded country. Small open areas along the way contain numerous buffalo droppings, indicating the passage of these animals through here in spring and early summer. You may spot an occasional bull at any time during the summer and early fall. At the 7.5 mi. mark you cross Calfee Creek, and just beyond the creek about 0.3 mi. is a N.P.S. patrol cabin. At 8.5 mi. there is a trail junction. Here the Miller Creek Trail forks to the east, leading to some very wild, seldom visited country. The Lamar River Trail crosses Miller Creek and continues along the Lamar River, mostly through unchanging scenery. There are populations of cutthroat and rainbow trout in the river, though the rainbow is seldom caught above the confluence of Soda Creek.

As you approach the meadows leading to Cold Creek Junction, the scenery changes. The Absaroka Range will appear to the southeast. The Cold Creek patrol cabin lies 0.5 mi. short of Cold Creek Junction, on the west side of the Lamar River. There are some fine campsites in the Cold Creek Junction area near the confluence of Cold Creek and the Lamar River. Cold Creek Junction makes an ideal spot in which to set up a base camp and plan a stay of several days. From here the Lamar River Trail continues 6 more miles to the Upper Lamar River patrol cabin, where it terminates; the Frost Lake Trail climbs 6 mi. up to the park boundary; the Mist Creek Trail leads over Mist Creek Pass to Pelican Springs and the Pelican Valley, and nearby Little Saddle Mountain offers a very rewarding climb. (Any travel away from established trails should be by experienced hikers, and permission must be obtained.)

The trail up to the Upper Lamar River patrol cabin follows the Lamar River on the north side and remains low in the valley, with prominent peaks rising on both sides. Saddle Mountain (10,670 ft.) lies to the north of the Upper Lamar River Trail, and may be climbed without too much difficulty by zigzagging up the slopes following open areas to the top. If you do not travel up the Upper Lamar River Trail, the Little Saddle Mountain (10,228 ft.) can be climbed, beginning from your camp at Cold Creek Junction. Both peaks offer almost the same view, which is magnificent. The climb up Little Saddle Mountain is slightly more difficult as there are fewer open areas to follow. From

Cold Creek Junction you cross the meadow, then start up the forested ridge. The first 1.5 mi. are heavily forested, but after you break through these dense woods the peak will become visible, and the remaining ascent to the top is quite easy. From the top of Little Saddle Mountain you command a spectacular 360° view. To the west across the Lamar River is Pelican Cone (9,648 ft.), with its fire lookout visible on top. Beyond Pelican Cone is a bird's-eye view of Yellowstone Lake. Portions of the Pelican Valley are also visible. To the northwest lies the Lamar Valley from where you began your hike. Rugged peaks reminiscent of Glacier National Park rise sharply to elevations of over 11,000 ft., Castor and Pollux to the southeast being the most prominent. Buffalo normally spend the summer in the high country, and you may spot a herd from the summit.

The Frost Lake Trail is another splendid side trip available from Cold Creek Junction. The trail's name is rather misleading, as it does not actually lead to Frost Lake, but passes within 1 mi. of it. Getting to the lake requires crossing U.S.F.S. land which is not shown on the U.S.G.S. topo map of Yellowstone. If Frost Lake is your main objective, it is wise to have a U.S.G.S. 15-min. map of Pelican Cone, 1959, to aid in locating the lake. The lake can be located by following the small tributary of Cold Creek which drains into it, but there is no trail.

The Frost Lake Trail provides a good view of Little Saddle Mountain from the Lamar River before entering the forest and beginning the steep climb up to the park boundary. About halfway up the trail you will pass through an area where there are still signs of a violent storm in 1964. Near the park boundary you will be approaching about

9,600 ft. and will command spectacular views of Castor Peak, Pollux Peak, and Notch Mountain. Close to the park boundary, a sign pointing to the west says "Frost Lake: 1 mile"; as there is no trail, it may be difficult to find without a map depicting U.S.F.S. land. There is a small lake at the park boundary which remains all summer. Even if you do not visit Frost Lake, the trip up to and across the park boundary is well worth the time and effort.

From Cold Creek Junction it is 11 mi. to Pelican Springs, following the Mist Creek Pass Trail. The hike is through dense forest all the way except for 1 meadow through which Mist Creek runs. Cold Creek and Mist Creek both contain populations of small cutthroat. From Pelican Springs it is 7 mi. out to the trailhead on the Fishing Bridge-East Entrance Road. (See *Pelican Creek-Astringent Creek Trail.*)

The Thunderer Cutoff Trail   (7.5 mi.)

Start from the trailhead 1 mi. northeast of Pebble Creek campground on the Tower-Northeast Entrance Road. The trail begins from near the confluence of Soda Butte and Amphitheater creeks; Abiathar Peak and Amphitheater Mountain—both over 10,800 ft.—are prominent to the northeast. The trail climbs almost 2,000 ft. over a series of sharp switchbacks to the north ridge of The Thunderer, so named for its apparent focus for thunderstorms. The Thunderer, at 10,558 ft., contains talus slopes and a number of impressive cliff bands at the north end. From the top of the saddle there is a magnificent view to the southeast of The Needle, a pinnacle which dominates the valley of Lower Cache Creek. The impressive "needle's eye" arch extends about 35 ft. above the rock ridge: a cross-country bushwhacking hike of about 3 mi. from the Cache Creek Trail is necessary to reach this. The trail descends sharply to Cache Creek 0.3 mi. south of Cache Creek patrol cabin.

Cache Creek Trail (16.6 mi.)

The Lamar River Trail 3.3 mi. south of the Soda Butte Creek Bridge is the starting point for this trail. The trail stays high above the north bank of Cache Creek until the 2 mi. mark, at which point Death Gulch is visible on the south side of the creek. The hydrogen sulphide gas from the vents in this gloomy gulch has caused the death of many animals over the years, from bears and coyotes to numerous smaller mammals. In certain wind conditions the gulch can be extremely dangerous, and hikers are warned against entering this area.

With Mt. Norris to the west and The Needle to the east, the trail continues upstream along Cache Creek, reaching the patrol cabin at the 11.3 mi. mark. Republic Pass is reached on the park boundary at about 10,000 ft. The Republic Creek Trail (U.S.F.S.) leads down the east side past an old mining site to Cooke City. There is also another trail (not shown on most maps), which continues up the middle fork of Cache Creek (extending beyond the Republic Pass turnoff) and crosses Crandall Pass at 9,920 ft. on the boundary, which provides access to the North Fork Crandall Creek Trail (U.S.F.S.). Jack Crandall was a prospector killed by Indians along Crandall Creek on July 1, 1870. His unmarked grave is located in the North Fork Crandall Creek area.

Miller Creek Trail
(and Side Trips From Upper Miller Creek)   (8.5 mi.)

Start at the Lamar River Trail, 8.5 mi. south of the Soda
Butte Creek Bridge (1 mi. south of Calfee Creek patrol
cabin). This trail leads up into a wild portion of the rugged
northern Absarokas, seldom visited. Miller Creek, which
contains some cutthroat, was named in 1880 by Park
Superintendent Norris for Adam "Horn" Miller, the dis-
coverer of Soda Butte, as a result of Miller's narrow escape
from Indians in 1870 when he descended this stream. The
Canoe Lake Trail, 1 mi. west of the patrol cabin, climbs
sharply up the ridge and leads to Canoe Lake and the park
boundary 4 mi. away. The lake, at 9,200 ft., is very narrow
and contains no fish. Timber Creek Trail (U.S.F.S.) leads
from the park boundary to the Sunlight Basin Road about
19 mi. away.

From the Miller Creek patrol cabin there is a trail which
continues up the creek to Bootjack Gap (9,180 ft.) on the
park boundary, 4 mi. from the cabin. This is quite steep
and rocky. Another trail from the cabin leads to the Hoodoo Basin area 7 mi. away. From the cabin, the Hoodoo
Trail climbs over 2,000 ft. to just north of Parker Peak
(10,203 ft.). It was north of Parker Peak that Superintendent Norris in 1880 discovered the remains of a strategic
Indian camp perched high on the grassy pass, with views of
all possible approaches for miles around. The camp, which
contained 40 decaying lodges, was apparently used by
Indians during the summer. Norris found the remains of
white men's blankets, bedding, china, and male and female
clothing as evidence of their raids.

The Hoodoo Basin was named for the "goblins" or

"hoodoos" that "inhabit" the area (the result of the many
eroded rock pinnacles in grotesque forms). From the basin,
the trail crosses the park boundary and follows the Absaroka Range a few miles before descending into the old Sunlight mining region (about 10 mi. from the boundary).
From here a dirt jeep road leads to the Sunlight Ranger
Station (U.S.F.S.). A 15-min. U.S.G.S. topo map of Sunlight Peak, 1956, is needed for travel in this area.

Specimen Ridge Trail   (17.5 mi.)

The starting point is east of Yellowstone River bridge on
Northeast Entrance Road, 0.9 mi. from Tower Junction. If
the petrified trees are your primary objective rather than a
cross-country hike, it is recommended that you park just
west of the Lamar River bridge (where a pullout is provided) and follow the west fork of Crystal Creek up to the
top of the ridge. The round-trip distance is only about 4 mi.
(though a steep climb of about 1,200 ft. is required), and
there are fine specimens on the sides and top of the ridge—
some 4 ft. in diameter.

From the trailhead, the trail follows the east side of the
Yellowstone River and Canyon for 2 mi., then slowly
climbs up to the ridge (a distance of 5 mi.). Yellowstone
contains the most extensive and remarkable petrified forest
in the world. The trees here extend over 40 sq. mi., a larger
area than any other known fossil forest. Most of them are
still standing upright, unlike those in California, Egypt, and
Arizona, whose noted Petrified Forest National Park consists of scattered, petrified driftwood. Finally, in addition
to the petrified tree trunks, thousands of fossilized imprints
of twigs, leaves, seeds, needles, and cones have been found

in the volcanic rocks of this region.

The "frozen" tree trunks you see standing upright are the ancient remains of a deciduous forest which existed 55 million years ago at an elevation of only 2,000 ft. There are oaks, maples, sycamores, dogwoods, hickories, walnuts, and chestnuts—similar to what you would find in North Carolina, for example, today. When volcanic activity began in the area, lava flows completely engulfed the forest; the buried trees absorbed silica from the ash and mud, and as a result were preserved. Scientists have discovered 27 layers of petrified trees in this area. After one volcanic eruption, thousands of years would pass before the soil and conditions allowed another forest to take hold and grow. Then another volcanic eruption would once again cover the forest, and the process would start again. Although 27 layers of successive forests have been discovered, there are estimates that perhaps 44 layers exist. The very hard and colorful trees of the top layers have withstood the processes of erosion, and as a result now stand exposed up to 15 ft. high in some places on the slopes. With binoculars it is possible to spot such trees from the Northeast Entrance Road near the Lamar River bridge. The most striking examples of layering are found on the north side of Specimen Ridge above the Lamar River Valley.

There are occasional naturalist-conducted hikes to the petrified trees on Specimen Ridge; the trip usually lasts from half to all day, and is an excellent way to get acquainted with the area. (For information, inquire at any of the park's Visitor Centers.) *Visitors are reminded that it is against the law to collect specimens, and violators risk severe penalties.*

The name Specimen Ridge seems appropriate when you consider the names of the streams that drain this region— Quartz, Agate, Crystal, Jasper, Amethyst, and Chalcedony creeks. In late summer, however, streams are hard to find (with the exception of Agate Creek). If you are traveling Specimen Ridge at this time of year you may need to take water with you, particularly if you plan to stay on top in open, rather dry country. During early summer you may spot a number of grizzlies in these open areas, so be alert. Amethyst Mountain is the trail's high point (9,614 ft.) at the 12 mi. mark. From here the trail begins a steady descent to the Lamar River, which you must ford to gain access to the Lamar River Trail. This leads across open country to the Soda Butte Creek bridge and the Northeast Entrance Road.

Wapiti Lake Trail   (14.5 mi.)

Start from Artist Point, reached via the spur road on the south rim of the canyon. You can also begin from the parking lot at the bridge across the Yellowstone River (on the Artist Point spur road). After leaving the Grand Canyon of Yellowstone, the Wapiti Lake Trail enters dense lodgepole forest that continues all the way to the lake. For this reason it is not highly recommended. If the Fern Lake area is your objective, it is suggested that you take the more scenic Pelican Creek or Astringent Creek trails beginning from Pelican Valley. Some people prefer to leave the Wapiti Lake Trail and explore many of the thermal areas of the Mirror Plateau (these are not reached by trail). With compass and topo map, experienced hikers who have permission may leave the Wapiti Lake Trail at Moss Creek and make a loop, exploring Whistler Geyser and Josephs Coat Springs, Coffee Pot Hot Springs, Rainbow Springs, and Hot Springs Basin group before rejoining the Wapiti Lake Trail.

The Cook-Folsom-Peterson Expedition of 1869 passed through here while exploring the Yellowstone region. These 3 men received very little recognition for their findings, as publishers refused to incorporate all their material for fear of being accused of exaggeration. However, the following year the Washburn party made their historic journey, and their reports were received with more respect. Wapiti Lake —small and in dense woods—is the source for Shallow Creek.

Mt. Washburn Trail   (3 mi.)

The top of Mt. Washburn can be reached by trail either from Dunraven Pass (5.6 mi. from the canyon on the Canyon-Tower Road) or by car along a dirt road from the Canyon-Tower Road 5 mi. north of Dunraven Pass. Cars are not allowed on the summit, but you can drive for about 1.5 mi. to a small parking area with a fine view (especially at sunset). Of the 2 routes to the summit, the dirt road is probably the easiest as it climbs gradually. Mt. Washburn, which rises to 10,243 ft., is composed largely of breccia. Its slopes are summer home for a large number of bighorn sheep, frequently spotted as you near the top. From the summit you will have a view of the Grand Canyon of Yellowstone (E), steam rising from Josephs Coat Springs and Whistler Geyser, and Hayden Valley and Yellowstone Lake to the south. Also visible on a clear day are the Tetons, Absarokas, and Gallatin Range. General Henry D. Washburn climbed the peak in August, 1870, in a successful attempt to locate the best route to Yellowstone Lake. Near the summit, you may notice glacial grooves and scratches which were caused by sheets of ice 800 ft. thick scraping against the mountainside. Notice how the high altitude disfigures the whitebark pine. A lookout is stationed atop the summit during the summer months.

Tower Falls Trail   (0.4 mi.)

The trail starts from The Tower Falls overlook. Tower Falls is one of Yellowstone's most popular attractions. Many have witnessed its 132 ft. plunge, but few take the new trail to the base. From here the falls looks completely different and very impressive. On a sunny morning, a rainbow frames the foot of the falls. Minarets, or "towers," extend above the brink for which the cataract was named by members of the 1870 Washburn party. Everyone wonders when the large boulder sitting on the brink will fall. Early pictures in 1872 show it at the same spot. It is believed that John Colter crossed the Yellowstone River near here in 1807.

Pelican Creek-Astringent Creek Loop Trail   (16.5, 11 mi.)

The trailhead is at the end of a short dirt road located on the north side of the Fishing Bridge-East Entrance Road, 3.3 mi. from Fishing Bridge (across from Squaw Lake).

Pelican Creek Trail

It is about 2 mi. before you emerge into spacious Pelican Valley. The area is ideal grizzly habitat and you will probably spot several droppings and diggings along the way. Make noise and remain alert as you traverse the valley. Coyotes are frequently sighted throughout the valley searching for small game. At the 3 mi. point you reach Pelican Creek and a junction with the old fire road used to provide access to forest fire areas. Pelican Creek moves along rather slowly. The water is not very cold and therefore makes poor drinking water. There are good populations of cutthroat in this stream, however. If you are making the loop hike, continue along the trail near the south side of the creek and do not cross at the bridge. As you walk through the Pelican Valley, you will see the Sulphur Hills in the distance (NW) and Pelican Cone Lookout (9,648 ft.) to the northeast. At the 4.5 mi. mark (1.5 mi. beyond the old road trail junction), you will come to an unnamed stream. A small waterfall is located here. Pelican Springs patrol cabin lies at the valley's far end (7 mi.). Directly across from the cabin (SE) is a small spring.

As you continue your loop hike, Raven Creek is crossed 1 mi. from Pelican Springs. (There are cutthroat trout here.) Another 0.7 mi. brings you to the junction of the trail leading to Pelican Cone Lookout. The climb up Pelican Cone (4.5 mi.) is about 1,600 ft. It affords a fine view of Yellowstone Lake to the southwest and Saddle Mountain to the east. At Pelican Creek you will come to the terminus of the old fire road. You have now traveled 9 mi. From this point on up Pelican Creek the trail is overgrown in many places, as this area receives very little travel. The orange trail markers will help guide you up the valley. At the 11 mi. mark you will come to a thermal area which consists of

the Mudkettles to the west and the Mushpots to the east.
The Mudkettles are the more interesting, consisting mainly
of a series of deep mudpots. Remember to be very careful
when near such thermal areas—stay off ground that appears
to be unstable. Another 3 mi. (14 mi. from the trailhead)
brings you to one of the most interesting thermal areas in
the Mirror Plateau. Located about 75 yds. to the east of the
trail, "Hot Springs" is actually a very large mud geyser in a
state of constant mild eruption, with occasional bursts of
up to 30 ft. (Near the headwaters of Pelican Creek, one of
the park's most notorious poachers, a man by the name of
Howell, was captured while skinning several buffalo he had
just slaughtered.)

About 1 mi. past the mud geyser the trail forks to the
left down to Pelican Creek and a meadow. Here you will
find a trail junction. To the north is Fern Lake patrol cabin
(*not* located on Fern Lake) 0.5 mi. away. Wapiti Lake is 4
mi. to the north. You have now reached the "top" of your
loop hike, unless you decide to continue to either of these
destinations. Broad Creek and the Astringent-Broad Creek
Trail are only 0.7 mi. away. Throughout your trip to
Pelican Creek you will have noticed a small but prominent
ridge to the west which separates Pelican Creek from
Broad and Astringent creeks. You are now about to cross it.

When you reach Broad Creek, you will actually be at the
Broad Creek-Astringent Creek trailhead, and signs are
posted here to that effect. Just to the north of the trail
junction the Fern Lake Trail leads across the creek to the
lake. There are populations of small rainbow further downstream, but here the fishing is very slow. Fern Lake, at 16.5

mi., lies deep in the forest at an elevation of 8,245 ft., with a wooded slope rising from the north shore. At the east end of the lake where the trail emerges from the forest there are several hot springs near the shore. There are no fish. The trail climbs up again from the lake, passes through an old burned area, then re-enters a forest. As you continue away from the lake (SW), you will pass through a meadow extending north to south, and 1.5 mi. from the east end of Fern Lake will come to the Ponuntpa Springs group. There is a fine meadow here, but the springs are mostly inactive and dried up.

Astringent Creek Trail

The Astringent Creek Trail, from Broad Creek near Fern Lake down to Pelican Creek, offers wild and beautiful scenery. At 1.2 mi. you will come to Tern Lake, which teems with various forms of birdlife—duck, geese, and quite probably trumpeter swan. The lake is very shallow, with marshy areas all around. (There are no fish in Fern, Tern, or White lakes.) Beyond the lake to the west is a ridge which has been burned over by a forest fire. The trail continues to follow Broad Creek through mostly open country. At 2.5 mi., White Lake will be to the west of the trail but only partially visible. The main body of the lake is about 0.5 mi. from the trail. White Lake is very similar to Tern Lake in that it is in open marshy surroundings and an ideal habitat for a great variety of birdlife. White Lake is the source for Broad Creek. The next creek you see at the 3 mi. mark will be Astringent Creek. From the moment you come to Astringent Creek until you enter the Pelican Valley you enjoy a spectacular display of wildflowers, especially during late July and early- to mid-August. The trail follows Astringent Creek through meadows literally painted with flowers: western yarrow (white), harebell (blue), fringed gentian (purple), Indian paintbrush (pink and red), arnica (yellow), larkspur (blue), lupine (blue and purple), and wild geranium (pink to lavender).

As you approach Pelican Valley the rounded shape of Lake Butte at 8,348 ft. appears directly to the south, and Mt. Chittenden (10,181 ft.) overlooks the valley to the southeast. On re-entering Pelican Valley, scan the hillsides for animals—you may spot a coyote searching for rodents. When you cross the old fire road bridge across Pelican Creek you will have come 8 mi. from the Astringent Creek trailhead at Broad Creek. It is another 3 mi. across Pelican Valley to the trailhead on the Fishing Bridge-East Entrance Road (across from Squaw Lake).

Jones Pass-Crow Creek Pass Trail   (13 mi.)

This trail has the same trailhead as Pelican Creek Trail. The dirt service road is followed for 3 mi. to Turbid Lake. From here the trail begins a climb of about 1,600 ft. up to Jones Pass, following Bear Creek much of the way. Just short of Jones Pass you will arrive at a trail junction. You can continue over the pass, descending Jones Creek in the Shoshone National Forest, or you can take the south fork, go over Crow Creek Pass, and descend Crow Creek. The first is the more scenic route. Jones Pass and Creek (on the east drainage) are named for Captain W. A. Jones of the U.S. Corps of Engineers, who first explored this region. In 1873,

Captain Jones led an important expedition through Yellow-stone, which took him over this pass—probably the first white man to cross it.

Jones Pass is similar to Bliss Pass in that the east slope is extremely steep, and the trail follows a series of switch-backs in a sharp descent of 1,000 ft. in 1.5 mi. From the top of the pass the view of the surrounding scenery is ter-rific. Mt. Chittenden and Cathedral Peak are 2 prominent peaks of the Absaroka Range to the north, the Jones Creek Valley lies below you to the east, and the cirque which contains Stonecup Lake is visible to the northeast. To the south, there are fine views of Yellowstone Lake.

If you continue over the pass you will follow Jones Creek for 11 mi. before it flows into the North Fork Sho-shone River at Sam Berry Meadow in Shoshone National Forest. From here the trail leads south along the river for 4 mi. to the Cody Road, 2 mi. from the East Entrance. (Note that for travel in this area you will need 15-min. maps of Pelican Cone, Wyo., and Sunlight Peak, Wyo.)

From Crow Creek Pass the trail descends Crow Creek for about 10 mi. and then turns south for 1 mi. along the North Fork Shoshone River before joining the Cody Road at the same spot. Silvertip Peak (10,659 ft.) and Giant Cas-tle Mountain (10,161 ft.) separate the Jones Creek drainage from that of Crow Creek.

Avalanche Peak Hike   (2 mi.)

Start from the first parking area west of Eleanor Lake on the Fishing Bridge-East Entrance Road (about 1.3 mi. west of Sylvan Pass). Although there is no maintained trail to the summit, this hike is certainly feasible and provides some magnificent scenery. Naturalist-conducted trips are occasionally made here during late summer; inquire at any Visitor Center for information. From the road you climb about 2,000 ft. in 2 mi. to the summit at 10,566 ft., passing through flower-laden alpine meadows along the way. Yellowstone Lake dominates the view from the summit, with distant mountain ranges visible on clear days.

SHORT HIKES FROM
CANYON VILLAGE AREA

The Canyon Village area offers the best range of short hikes available to the day hiker anywhere in the park. Both rims of the Canyon itself contain trails that offer breathtaking views. An easy trail of only 0.1 mi. runs to the brink of the Upper Falls. A short spur road leads there, beginning from the Canyon-Lake Road about 2 mi. south of Canyon Junction. There are also trails to the brink and foot of the Lower Falls, but they are quite strenuous. The short hike to the brink of the Lower Falls begins from the one-way loop road on the north rim, and consists of a number of switchbacks. Uncle Tom's Trail, which begins from the Artist Point spur road on the south rim, leads to near the foot of the Lower Falls, and provides a wonderful view of the falls from the bottom of the canyon. This particular trail was originally built in 1903 by Thomas Richardson, at which time it consisted of a number of rope ladders and was quite dangerous.

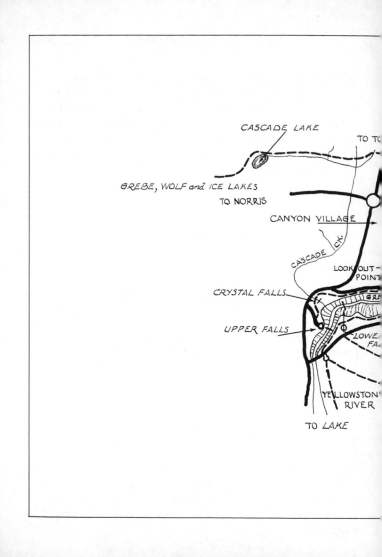

CANYON AREA

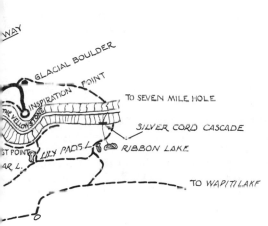

LS

WAY

GLACIAL BOULDER

INSPIRATION POINT

THE YELLOWSTONE

TO SEVEN MILE HOLE

SILVER CORD CASCADE

ST POINT LILY PADS L. RIBBON LAKE

AR L.

TO WAPITI LAKE

Crystal Falls-Upper Falls Trail   (0.6 mi.)

Start from the parking lot on the Upper Falls spur road.
There is a bridge across a small stream: the trail begins on
the northwest side of the stream (trailhead not marked).
The first 200 yds. bring you to the edge of the canyon that
Cascade Creek flows through, and a fine view of Crystal
Falls (129 ft.). Here the trail forks; the left fork is the
North Rim Trail, leading to the edge of the Grand Canyon
and around to the Lower Falls brink trail; the right fork
continues down to the Yellowstone River and the foot of
the Upper Falls. If at all possible, take the time to walk up
the left fork of the trail the few 100 yds. to the small
footbridge that crosses Cascade Creek above Crystal Falls.
Throughout the little gorge between the bridge and falls
you may be able to spot the aquatic water ouzel, one of the
most fascinating birds to be found anywhere.

From the fork in the trails you should follow the right
fork to gain access to the foot of the Upper Falls. There are
several impressive views of Crystal Falls, discovered and
named by members of the Washburn Party in 1870. After
plunging over Crystal Falls, Cascade Creek flows only a
short distance farther before it empties into the Yellowstone River, easily visible below you to the east. The trail
continues to wind downhill. On reaching the banks of the
Yellowstone River, it carries on upstream to near the foot
of the Upper Falls. Here the white spray of the falls reaches
out in every direction, and its seemingly slow-motion action
is almost hypnotic. During June, over 64,000 gallons of
water per second plunge over the brinks of the Lower and
Upper falls. This flow is reduced to 5,000 gallons per second by autumn. In winter the falls are still active, but are

hidden behind a large ice and snow cone extending from brink to foot. From the foot of the falls you must turn around and follow the trail back out, as there is no safe path leading on up to the brink. Occasionally, people climb up the ridge to the brink; not only is this dangerous, but it rapidly accelerates erosion.

Ribbon Lake-Clear Lake Loop Trail   (4.2 mi.)

Start from Artist Point at the end of the spur road. Try to visit the area several times—at sunrise, midday, sunset, and by moonlight. In this way you will really come to know the beauty of the Lower Falls and the canyon. Indians referred to this section of the Yellowstone River as "the river with yellow, vertical walls." The park is named for the yellow walls of the Grand Canyon. Basically the canyon is constructed of rhyolite softened by water and hot gases, and therefore more easily carved than unaltered rhyolite. The Yellowstone River channel is being continually deepened by the forces of the raging river, which carries silt and stones to accelerate the cutting process.

The Lower and Upper falls were created because the layers of basalt and extremely hard rhyolite at the lips of these cataracts have yielded very slowly to erosion as compared to the softer rhyolite. The yellows and oranges of the canyon's walls and pinnacles are the result of the oxides of various minerals contained in the rhyolite.

From Artist Point, the trail follows the rim of the canyon for 0.5 mi. before bending off into the forest. If you are fortunate enough to be along this stretch at sunset, you will see an unforgettable sight. The flaming reds of the canyon on the north side are particularly striking. You can spot Mt. Washburn on your right (10,243 ft.) with its fire lookout tower on top. The next peak west from Mt. Washburn (to your left) is Dunraven Peak, (9,900 ft.), named in honor of the Earl of Dunraven, who visited the park in 1874 and published many works abroad about Yellowstone. To the left of Dunraven Peak is Hedges Peak, named after Cornelius Hedges, the member of the 1870 Washburn party who first proposed that Yellowstone should be established as a national park. West of Dunraven is Observation Peak (9,397 ft.).

At .75 mi. you come to Lilypad Lake, where you will notice a sulphureous odor from the small outlet at the southeast end of the lake. Just beyond Lilypad Lake there is a trail junction. The left fork leads to Ribbon Lake, 1.3 mi. away, the right, to Clear Lake and out to the Artist Point spur road. The 1.3 mi. walk to Ribbon Lake is through a forest where wildflowers abound. There are also a number of small ponds.

As the trail nears Ribbon Lake, you are above it. When you descend to the lake, you reach another trail junction, having come 2 mi. It is possible to follow this trail and loop back to the Chittenden bridge on the Artist Point spur road, but this is not recommended for a day hike because beautiful Clear Lake is bypassed. The trail to the left continues along Ribbon Lake, crosses its outlet (which flows into the Grand Canyon as Silver Cord Cascade), and terminates along the canyon rim. Ribbon Lake contains a growth of brown algae, hence the rusty color. After crossing this stream, the trail winds up to the canyon's edge for another spectacular view of the Yellowstone River below, several mountain peaks to the north and northwest, and a partial view of Silver Cord Cascade. Extensive meadows border both Ribbon Lake and the unnamed lake just to its northeast. Chances of sighting moose and elk in these meadows are excellent during early morning and later afternoon. (There are no fish in either lake.)

From Ribbon Lake you follow the trail 1.3 mi. back to the trail junction near Lilypad Lake. As you proceed on the left fork (heading south), only a few 100 yds. from the trail junction you will notice considerable thermal activity to the left of the trail. As there is a boiling mudpot here, be very careful not to approach it too closely. From this point on to Clear Lake (0.5 mi.), you will pass a number of boiling mudpots, hot springs, and fumaroles.

Clear Lake is fed by cold springs and contains no fish. After passing the lake, the trail emerges from the forest into an extensive open area which lasts the rest of the way. Just above Clear Lake the trail forks; there will probably be no sign here, but the left fork continues out to near Chittenden bridge, and the right fork takes the shorter route out to the Uncle Tom's Trail parking lot on the Artist Point spur road. After turning right at the junction, you will come on yet another lovely view of the canyon and of the familiar mountain peaks in the distance (L to R: Observation Peak, Hedges Peak, Dunraven Peak, and Mt. Washburn). You may spot an osprey soaring over the canyon. The osprey population has suffered greatly in recent years as a result of DDT and other residual pesticides. Only a few years ago it was possible to see more than a dozen at a time over the canyon, and to count up to 20 nests on the canyon walls.

The wildflowers along this route, particularly in June, are spectacular. You can pick out the glacier lily, shooting star, balsam root, mariposa lily, harebell, and bitterroot, to mention only a few. The area is also ideal habitat for both grizzly and black bear. The grizzly will often spend hours digging for rodents and for the bulbous roots of glacier lilies. Chances are fairly good of spotting a black, especially in the spring; a grizzly is less likely, as the terrain is too close to roads and people.

The trail continues a short way further before the Artist Point spur road comes into view below you. You emerge opposite the Uncle Tom's Trail parking lot.

Glacial Boulder to Seven-Mile Hole   (5.1 mi.)

The starting point is Glacial Boulder on Inspiration Point spur road, located on the north rim of the Grand Canyon. Although the destination is Seven-Mile Hole, the total distance is only 5.1 mi. if you begin from Glacial Boulder, a huge mass of stone deposited by moving glaciers during the Wisconsin Ice Age.

The first 1.2 mi. of this hike are highly recommended, as there are splendid views into the Grand Canyon, and also of Silver Cord Cascade, which plunges some 800 ft. down the south wall of the canyon; the falls are in a crevice partially hidden from view except from directly across the canyon at this point. Beyond, the trail swings away from the canyon's edge for another 1.3 mi. before beginning the sharp descent to the bottom. It winds all the way down to the Yellowstone River at the foot of the canyon where Sulphur Creek empties into it. Along the way you will notice signs of thermal activity. The fishing in this stretch of the river is outstanding; as a result, this portion of the hike is popular with avid fishermen who do not mind an extremely strenuous hike back out. A new trail to "Three-Mile Hole" is scheduled to open very soon, which will lead to the bottom of the canyon from near the Silver Cord Cascade viewpoint. (For information, inquire at the Canyon Ranger Station.) Unfortunately, littering problems have occurred in the past at the bottom of the canyon; *please pack out everything that you pack in.*

Grebe Lake Trail (3 mi.)

Grebe Lake parking area on Canyon-Norris Road, 3 mi. from Canyon Junction, is the starting point for this trail. This particular day hike is rather popular—partly due to the fishing at Grebe Lake, but also because of the beauty of the lake and vicinity. The entire 3 mi. runs through dense lodgepole pine forest.

At one time a road led most of the way to Grebe Lake, but it is now closed to all vehicles. At the 2 mi. mark be sure to take the trail that forks left, and not continue down the road. After 3 mi. of lodgepole, Grebe Lake is a welcome sight as you emerge from the forest. On the east, south, and west shores are meadows, in which you can usually see wildlife during early morning and late afternoon. The lake is at an elevation of 8,020 ft. and is the source of the Gibbon River, which flows from its western end.

A pair of trumpeter swan often spend most of the summer here. Grebe Lake is also one of the last strongholds of the arctic grayling in Yellowstone Park. Competition from such artificially introduced species as the rainbow and brown trout has limited their distribution to Grebe, Wolf, and Ice lakes, and portions of the Gibbon River connecting these. The arctic grayling does not compete well with other species, and in an attempt to preserve this beautiful fish, the park has established a catch-and-release regulation: No graylings may be kept, regardless of size.

Remnants of an old fish hatchery can still be seen at the eastern end of the lake where a small stream enters it. Here, in early June during spawning season, thousands of grayling race back and forth. (The grayling is easily distinguished from other trout by its small mouth and large, beautifully colored dorsal fin.)

In the Grebe Lake area you should be extra alert for signs of grizzly bear. In recent years sightings have grown to be rather common, especially during spring and early summer. A clean and odor-free camp is a must. Note that mosquitoes are extremely thick in the Grebe and Cascade lakes area during June and July, so be sure to carry insect repellent.

Cascade Lake Trail   (2.8 mi.)

Start at Canyon-Norris Road, 0.5 mi. from Canyon Junction. The Cascade Lake hike, like Grebe Lake, is a very popular day hike for those visiting the canyon area. However, unlike the Grebe Lake Trail, Cascade Lake offers varied scenery. You will follow Cascade Creek most of the way, passing through several meadows and open areas in addition to stretches of lodgepole.

As you emerge from the forest into a large meadow, you will see the lake at the far western end. Moose are often spotted in the marshy areas here and grizzlies, too, in spring and early summer.

Cascade Lake contains a population of cutthroat trout and arctic grayling, but they are normally not easy to catch. The lake itself lies between 2 mountains—Observation Peak

(NW) and Hedges Peak (NE). Although there is no maintained trail up Hedges Peak, an easy route to the summit
may be picked out by studying the slopes of the mountain
from the lake. The first part of the climb runs through
dense woods, but soon the trail emerges into the open, with
spectacular views toward the canyon and Hayden Valley as
well as of Cascade Lake itself.

Glacial Boulder to Washburn Hot Springs   (4 mi.)

The trailhead is at Glacial Boulder on the Inspiration Point
Road, which begins from Canyon Village. From Glacial
Boulder the trail enters lodgepole pine, and provides magnificent views of the Grand Canyon and Silver Cord Cascade. It then runs through dense lodgepole until Washburn
Hot Springs is reached at the 4 mi. mark. At the southern
base of Mt. Washburn is a group of interesting hot springs,
one of which is Inkpot Spring. There are also some impressive mudpots here. These springs can easily be seen from
the Canyon-Tower Road on a pullout near Dunraven Pass,
and may be reached from there. The forest is dense, making
for a difficult 2 mi. trip.

Appendices

A NOTE ABOUT THE TRAIL SYSTEM

In future years the National Park Service in Yellowstone will revise the trail system to include 3 classes (A, B, and C) of trails pertaining to maintenance:

Class A – Major trails – Routes marked, improved, and maintained for foot and horseback traffic. Includes necessary bridges, drainages, and 36 in. maximum tread.

Class B – Minor Trails – Routes marked, improved, and maintained to accommodate foot and horseback traffic, but of an overall lower construction standard. A maximum 24 in. tread.

Class C – Wilderness Trails – Routes will be marked, but unimproved except for clearing (and some work on dangerous areas). These trails should be used by experienced wilderness travelers only.

Most of Yellowstone's backcountry trails will be maintained as Class B trails. However, some of the trails contained in this book will undoubtedly become Class C trails. When making your plans and obtaining a backcountry use permit, you should get information about current trail conditions.

BRIEFED BOATING REGULATIONS

U.S. DEPARTMENT OF THE INTERIOR
NATIONAL PARK SERVICE
Yellowstone National Park, Wyoming 82190

CODE OF FEDERAL REGULATIONS, TITLE 36

Safety Suggestions

- Watch the weather; storms may arise suddenly.
- Water temperatures are extremely cold, and safe exposure time in the water is short.
- Small boats should always stay close to shore.
- All boats should seek shelter during heavy winds.
- Do not overload your boat.
- Know and observe the rules of the road.

(A complete copy of the boating regulations may be obtained at any ranger station.)

PERMITS – No privately-owned vessel shall be placed or operated upon the waters of Yellowstone National Park without a permit from the Superintendent. This permit (sticker) shall be placed on the port (left) side of the vessel, approximately one foot forward of the stern.

SPECIAL PERMIT – A special permit is *required* for all vessels traveling into either the South or Southeast arms of Yellowstone Lake. This permit describes the 5 mile per hour zones and the hand-propelled watercraft zones. The permit shall be returned to any ranger station within 24 hours after completion of the trip.

REMOVAL OF BOATS – All privately-owned boats and boat trailers will not be permitted in the park prior to May 1 and must be removed by November 1.

RESTRICTED LANDING AREAS – Prior to July 1, the landing of any vessel on the shore of Yellowstone Lake between Trail Creek and Beaverdam Creek is prohibited, except upon written permission of the Superintendent. The beaching, launching, or mooring of any vessel on the shore of Yellowstone Lake within the Bridge Bay Marina and Lagoon is prohibited except at the docks or piers provided. The beaching, launching, or mooring of vessels is also prohibited along the shore of Yellowstone Lake from the mouth of Little Thumb Creek to Grant Village Marina except at the piers and docks located within the Grant Village Launch Lagoon and Marina.

CLOSED WATERS – All waterborne craft of every type or description are prohibited on Sylvan Lake, Eleanor Lake, Twin Lakes, Beach Springs Lagoon; and are prohibited on all park streams except the channel between Lewis Lake and Shoshone Lake, which is open only to hand-propelled vessels.

MOTORBOAT ZONES – Motor-driven vessels are permitted on Lewis Lake. Motor-driven vessels are permitted on Yellowstone Lake except in the southernmost 2 mi. of the South and Southeast arms and the westernmost 2 mi. of the Flat Mountain Arm. These zones are marked by buoys.

MOTORBOAT 5 MILE PER HOUR ZONES – A special permit is *required* for motorboats to enter the areas designated as 5 mile per hour zones—the northernmost 5 mi. of both the South and Southeast arms. These zones are marked by monuments and buoys and a speed of 5 miles per hour shall not be exceeded. Vessels 16 ft. and longer shall proceed no closer than 0.25 mi. from the shoreline, of the South and Southeast arms, except to load or unload passengers, or while moored when passengers are ashore.

The disturbance in any manner or by any means of the birds inhabiting or nesting on either of the islands designated as "Molly Islands" in the Southeast arm of Yellowstone Lake is prohibited; nor shall any vessel approach the shoreline of said islands within 0.25 mi.

These restrictions shall not apply to craft operated for administrative purposes or in emergencies.

HAND-PROPELLED WATERS – Hand-propelled vessels may be operated in all park waters except those excluded under "Closed Waters."

LAUNCHING – Boats transported by vehicles must be launched and removed from the waters only at designated launching sites.

LIFESAVING EQUIPMENT – All vessels shall carry a U.S. Coast Guard approved life preserver for each person on board. Lifesaving devices required on all vessels shall be in good and serviceable condition and shall be so placed as to be readily accessible.

LIGHTS REQUIRED – Every motorboat when underway from sunset to sunrise shall carry and exhibit lights prescribed for the applicable class of motorboat by your state or by the U.S. Coast Guard.

SIGNALING DEVICES – Motorboats shall be provided with an efficient whistle and/or other sound-producing device as prescribed for each class of motorboat.

RULES OF THE ROAD – The Statutory Rules of the Road which have been enacted by Congress to prevent collision of vessels must be followed by all operators.

ACCIDENTS – A report of collision, accident, fire, or other casualty that results in property damage or any personal injury or death to any person must be made by each operator of vessels involved to the Superintendent or his representatives as soon as possible, and in any event within 24 hours. This report does not relieve the responsibility of making boating accident reports as may be required by states and/or the U.S. Coast Guard. Any operator involved in an accident shall also give in writing his name, address, and identification of his vessel to any person injured and/or to the owner of any property damaged.

OTHER SAFETY REQUIREMENTS – All vessels, except motorboats of Classes "2" and "3" shall be equipped with oars or paddles when underway.

No vessel, while underway, shall carry more than a safe capacity load in persons and/or total weight, taking into consideration water and weather conditions, hull configuration, and intended use.

All vessels of open construction shall carry a suitable bailing bucket, in addition to whatever bilge pumps or automatic bailing devices with which they may be equipped.

No vessel shall be operated in excess of 5 miles per hour within designated marinas.

WATER SANITATION – The draining, dumping, or discharging of wastes or refuse, including human wastes, into the waters from any vessel is prohibited.

All vessels shall have a waste receptacle aboard. Receptacles shall be emptied only into facilities provided at docks.

INSPECTIONS – The Superintendent or his authorized representatives may at any time stop or board any vessel to examine documents, licenses and/or permits relating to operation of the vessel and to inspect such vessel to determine compliance with regulations.

BOAT TRAILERS – Trailers or boats on trailers may not be parked within Yellowstone National Park for a period longer than fourteen (14) days.

CAMPING AND PICNICKING – Camping and picnicking are permitted at designated sites along the shores of Yellowstone Lake, provided that a permit is obtained in advance. Permits and maps of these sites may be obtained free of charge at any ranger station.

NOTES

NATURAL FIRE IN YELLOWSTONE

It is amazing how efficiently nature performs when we allow her to do so. Take forest fires, for example. It has been found that some plants and trees (such as the beautiful aspen) depend upon fire for their existence. Or what about fire and . . . fish? Nutrients in Yellowstone Lake have diminished 68% since 1884! Without fires in the lake drainage, many nutrients fail to reach the lake's waters. Less nutrients mean less food for the cutthroat, and so fewer cutthroat trout.

The important role that fire plays as an ecological force in Yellowstone ecosystems is being recognized and further studied. At the present time approximately 30% of Yellowstone's backcountry is designated as "free-burn" zones where naturally caused fires will be allowed to burn. As a result it is imperative that hikers check with rangers for current conditions before planning a trip into one of these regions. As of this writing, free-burn zones include portions of the Mirror Plateau and Two Ocean Plateau.

THE HOWARD EATON TRAIL

This trail was named for the famous horseman and early Yellowstone guide. In general, the trail parallels the Grand Loop Road and covers about 150 miles. Most of the trail is no longer maintained, though it is still fairly well marked. Due to the trail's close proximity to roads and to lack of maintenance, descriptions of areas along it have not been included.

However, some portions of the trail make for ideal day hikes. Some recommended segments for day hikers include from Glen Creek to Mammoth Hot Springs; from Indian Creek to Glen Creek; and from Blacktail Pond to Garnet Hill.

OFF-TRAIL TRAVEL

This book is certainly not a guide to *all* of Yellowstone's backcountry. In fact, the park's 1,000 miles of trails traverse only a portion of its 3,472 square miles. Those who enjoy traveling cross-country with compass and topo map have the opportunity of exploring seldom-visited mountain-tops, lakes, waterfalls, streams and thermal areas.

It is the opinion of this writer that such areas should be excluded from the pages of a trail guide, in order to preserve the mystique and feeling of discovery which accompanies present-day explorers today in much the same fashion that it did Colter, Bridger and other early explorers of the Yellowstone.

It must be emphasized that off-trail travel is for the expert backpacker only, and special permission must be received from park rangers before embarking on such a trip!

Field Notes

Field Notes

Field Notes

Field Notes

Field Notes

Field Notes

Field Notes